ROBERT CROFT BA, MIFA is the
County Archaeological Officer for
Somerset County Council

MICHAEL ASTON BA, FSA, MIFA is
Reader in Archaeology at Bristol University
and was the first County Archaeologist for
Somerset.

Front Cover Illustrations:
Wells Cathedral *(left)*, Wedmore *(right)*

Rear Cover Illustration:
Porlock Weir

This photograph, taken during the extreme drought conditions of the summer of 1976, shows the grassland around **EAST QUANTOXHEAD** was parched yellow and the ripening cereal crops give the whole scene an unusual golden colour. The low sunlight throws shadows of the trees across the fields. This area is part of the Quantock Hills Area of Outstanding Natural Beauty. In the middle distance is the St Mary's Church and Court House, the manor house of the Luttrell family since the thirteenth century. Beyond is Kilve Pill and the Bristol Channel.

SOMERSET
from the air

Robert Croft and
Michael Aston

Published by Somerset County Council
Design & artwork by Peter Webb
Printed by Hammett & Co. Ltd, Taunton

© Somerset County Council 1993

ISBN 0 86183 215 9

Few of us ever have the opportunity to take a 'bird's-eye view' of our local area, yet seen from the air, our towns and country-side take on a new and fascinating perspective. Somerset's rich landscape and historic heritage is exceptionally well-suited to study through aerial photography. This book brings together a selection of recent material to illustrate the character of the county and the changes which are taking place within it.

The County Council holds the largest collection of aerial photographs in Somerset, and these are widely-used by the local authorities, consultants and local people in connection with work on many environmental and planning matters.

I welcome this new publication in the belief that it will contribute to our knowledge and understanding of this beautiful county and its history.

Ralph Clark,
Chairman, Somerset County Council

CONTENTS

Chapter 6
FIELDS and FARMS . . . . **56 - 63**

Chapter 7
TOWNS and VILLAGES . . . . **64 - 85**

Chapter 8
MONASTIC SITES and CASTLES . . . . **86 - 95**

Aerofilms:

Pages 20, 21, 41, 53(upper), 65, 75, 77(upper), 79, 100, 108, 112, 117(lower), 118

M A Aston:

Pages 4/5, 28, 77(third)

S Banks (Pottery illustrations):

Page 49

Cambridge University Collection:

Front Cover(right), Pages 15(upper), 29, 33, 35, 46/47, 50, 54, 59, 67, 68, 81, 86/87, 90/91, 93, 95, 99(upper), 104

Crown Copyright:

Pages 25(lower), 58(lower)

Fleet Air Arm Museum, Yeovilton:

Page 111

Geonex UK Ltd:

Pages 18/19, 22/23, 24, 30/31, 99(lower), 113, 114/115, 117(upper), 119, Rear Cover

Frances Griffith:

Pages 17, 23, 25(upper), 40(upper), 43(lower), 48(upper & lower), 49, 52(upper), 55(upper), 61(upper), 71, 77(lower), 88(upper), 94(upper), 101, 105

Illustrated London News Photographic Library:

Page 53 (lower)

RCHME National Monuments Record Air Photography:

Page 89

Geoff Roberts:

Front Cover(left), Pages 34(lower), 55(lower), 110(middle)

Somerset Archaeological & Natural History Society (Engravings):

Pages 91, 98(lower)

Somerset County Council:

Pages 42(upper), 58(upper), 60(upper), 60(lower left), 62/63, 73(lower), 77(second), 88(lower left), 92, 94(lower), 96/97(lower), 102, 110(lower)

Somerset County Council Vertical Photographs 1971:

Pages 15(lower), 43(upper), 56, 60(lower right), 61(lower), 70, 72, 73(upper), 78, 80, 82, 83, 96/97(upper), 98(upper), 103, 109

Somerset County Council Vertical Photographs 1981:

Page 74

Millie Thompson (Illustration):

Page 55

Peter Webb (Illustrations):

Pages 34, 69, 74, 79, 97, 105

West Air Photography:

Pages 34(upper), 36, 38/39, 44/45, 51, 66, 76, 84/85, 107, 110(upper), 116(upper & lower)

Robert Winn:

Pages 26, 52(lower)

The Authors would particularly like to thank Russell Lillford, Ken Brown, Robert Dunning, David Bromwich and Chris Webster for their help and advice; Sarah Bisson and Christine Palmer for their typing skills and Peter Webb for the design.

ACCESS TO SITES:

Many of the sites and buildings illustrated in this book are on private land and public access may be limited.

GAZETTEER

Minehead

Cheddar

Wells

Glastonbury

Bridgwater

Watchet

Taunton

Wellington

Ilchester

Yeov

Chard

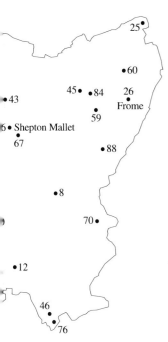

INTRODUCTION

Aerial photographs provide a unique and unusual view of the towns and countryside which we cherish and enjoy. An aerial photograph records a scene at a particular point in time and the collection reproduced in this book provides many examples of change and development within the county.

HISTORY OF AERIAL PHOTOGRAPHY IN SOMERSET

Aerial photography was difficult until developments in photographic technology made it possible to have easily portable cameras and stable photographic materials. Some of the earliest aerial photographs were taken at the turn of the century out of balloons or from early aircraft. It was the activities of early pioneers such as Major W G Allen or O G S Crawford in the 1930s, particularly in Wiltshire and Oxfordshire, which showed the value of aerial photography as a tool for researching the history of the landscape. All early photography was taken using glass negatives and consequently when the photographs do survive the detail and clarity of the prints is usually very good. There are a few 1940s and 1950s images of the county but it is not until the 1960s that many photographs are available of the towns and villages.

The main sources for early aerial photographs are given on page 120 but it is important to note that most of the photography carried out between 1950 and 1970 was oblique black and white photography done by private and commercial flyers such as Aerofilms. For archaeologists, some photography was undertaken by Cambridge University and the Royal Commission on the Historical Monuments of England, and examples of their work are included in this book.

TYPES OF AIR PHOTOGRAPHS

Two main types of aerial photograph are used in this book: **vertical**, that is looking straight down so that the view is like a map, and **oblique**, which is a bird's-eye view similar to looking out of an airliner or from a high building. Each type has a particular value to the researcher and they are used for a range of different purposes from survey to advertising.

Vertical photographs

These are the most common type of photograph used by government departments, local authorities, institutions and agencies for studying land. One of the main uses for large scale vertical photography, often at 1:2500 scale, is for map making, but in spite of their appearance vertical photographs are not maps as they do not record things at an exact scale. The surface of the earth is not flat and the photograph records all images seen by the camera without taking account of the changes in the vertical height of buildings or the countryside. Many vertical photographs are printed at a scale of approximately 1:10,000 and can be readily compared with Ordnance Survey maps of the same scale. Vertical aerial photographs usually cover large areas and when taken in overlapping runs they can be used for stereoscopic viewing. There are several advantages in using stereoscopic photographs, principally to enable plotting and interpretation of physical features to be undertaken with accuracy rather than guesswork. Stereoscopic viewing enables photographs to be viewed in an apparent '3D' image. There is a marked vertical exaggeration of changes in the ground level and this can be particularly useful to the researcher interested in plotting earthworks or changes in ground level. Simple pocket stereoscopes are perfectly adequate for most studies and can be used for looking at all types of site such as archaeological remains, field systems, the countryside and towns and villages.

Somerset has four main sources of vertical aerial photographs which cover most, if not all, of the county. The earliest photographs which are available for reference were taken by the Royal Air Force in 1946-7 as part of their national air survey. Earlier photographs taken in c.1940 by the German Luftwaffe exist for the county, but these are not available for reference locally. Some of the 1946-7 series of photographs are available at the Local History Library at Taunton Castle, Taunton, and a complete set is held by the RCHME. Several of these early RAF photographs are reproduced in this book and they provide an interesting illustration of the changes that have taken place in the county since the

Second World War. This particular set is very useful for archaeological surveys because it was taken with low sunlight and this picks out earthworks very clearly.

The most comprehensive coverage of the county is held by Somerset County Council and this includes county-wide runs which date from 1971, 1981 and 1992 at a scale of 1:10,000. In addition to the main series there are several part-sets of photographs which date mainly from the 1970s and 1980s including several thousand prints at 1:2500 scale used by the Ordnance Survey for map revision. Other part-sets exist for areas such as the Somerset Levels and Moors or Exmoor. This material is available for reference and further details of sources are given on page 120.

Oblique photographs

Most of the photographs used in this book are oblique, where the camera was at an angle to the ground and the result is that the photograph is much easier to interpret than a vertical image. Oblique photographs are particularly useful for picking out archaeological earthworks.

*The **oblique** photograph above shows the earthworks of the deserted settlement at Little Marston (West Camel).*
*The **vertical** photograph below shows Ham Hill to the left (see page 52) and Montacute to the right (see pages 104-105)*

ARCHAEOLOGICAL SITES AND AERIAL PHOTOGRAPHS

Archaeological and historic sites provide a great deal of evidence of the heritage of the county. Such sites are often difficult to interpret at ground level but when viewed from above their extent and character is much more obvious. The information recorded on the photograph will vary depending upon the time of year the photograph was taken.

Recent weather conditions can influence such things as waterlogging of the soil, snow cover over earthwork sites and the parching of crops due to drought conditions.

The three main sources of information about archaeological sites are:

Cropmarks

These occur where variations in soil depth and moisture within the soil cause plants to ripen at different rates across a field. Buried structures can affect the rate of growth and ripening of crops. Where there are buried pits and ditches the greater depth of topsoil will provide more plant nutrients giving a taller crop. The additional reserve of moisture in the topsoil results in the crop ripening later. Shallow soils over buried stonework give the opposite effect. An illustration of what can occur within a field under crop is shown in the diagram below. There are of course many other factors which affect the presence or absence of a cropmark; the individual microclimate within the field, the amount of rain which has fallen through the growing season and also the crop type. Some crops show up archaeological features much better than others and even after many years of careful monitoring and reconnaissance it is very difficult to predict when a crop mark will appear. After prolonged dry periods during drought conditions such as those which occurred in 1989, *parchmarks* can occur in grass which can result in the identification of buried remains.

Earthworks and Shadow Sites

The shadows cast by earthworks in low sunlight can provide a useful guide to changes in the landscape. There are many types of archaeological site which are difficult to see at ground level but when viewed from the air the shape and plan of the remains becomes extremely clear. This is particularly true of earthwork sites such as medieval villages and ploughed-out field systems (see pages 59 and 58). It is only under ideal lighting conditions that some subtle earthworks can be seen from the air. Low sunlight in the early morning or evening during the summer months can pick out the variations in relief and these *shadow sites* can best be seen throughout the day during the winter months.

Soil Marks

In certain conditions buried archaeological remains are being actively eroded by modern agricultural methods and where this occurs archaeological features such as ditches or banks can show as a variety of soil colours during ploughing. Such sites are referred to as *soil marks* .

THE USES OF AERIAL PHOTOGRAPHS IN EDUCATION AND RESEARCH

Aerial photographs are widely recognised as being an essential tool for research and education and recently there has been an increasing demand from students and teachers for access to aerial photographs of Somerset. The County Council is currently compiling a database which gives details of the main sources of aerial photography which are held in public and private collections. The National Curriculum has identified aerial photographs as a valuable source of information for several of the Key stages in educational attainment. Photographs of many of the main towns and some of the larger villages have been included in this book to help satisfy this demand for aerial photographs. There are several thousand other photographs available for study in the collections listed in the Sources section on page 120.

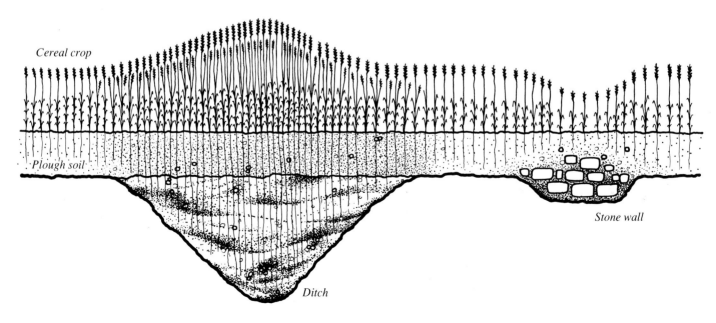

Cereal crop

Plough soil

Ditch

Stone wall

Historic Landscape Surveys

Archaeological and historic sites did not exist in isolation, they were surrounded by their contemporary road patterns and land uses. Any landscape contains a variety of sites and features of different periods and this 'palimpsest' (a re-use of the landscape by successive generations) can best be appreciated from the air. (See Minehead North Hill, page 22).

Within Somerset several detailed archaeological and historic landscape surveys have been undertaken in recent years with funding coming from a variety of sources, notably English Heritage and The Royal Commission on the Historical Monuments of England. All of these surveys have made extensive use of existing aerial photographs of the county. In some instances new photography has been commissioned to provide a reference point against which such things as agricultural activity can be measured. This is particularly true of the Somerset Levels and Moors area. Since 1989 a programme of aerial reconnaissance has been undertaken by Frances Griffith to look for and record archaeological sites. This work is funded by the RCHME and several hundred previously unrecorded sites have been discovered. Two interesting examples are Castlemans Hill, Trull (see photograph below) and additions to the extensive cropmark sites near Chedzoy (see page 48).

Anyone interested in finding out more about the material available for their area should contact the National Monuments Record Air Photography Unit, Cambridge University Collection and the County Sites and Monuments Record.

The value of aerial photography has often been underestimated in the past as a research tool, but almost all modern land-use mapping, environmental surveys and engineering works now use aerial photography to help with projects. The designation of Environmentally Sensitive Areas (ESAs) in The Somerset Levels and Moors, Exmoor and the Blackdown Hills will require careful monitoring by government agencies. Aerial photographs will be one of the main means used to ensure that this work is carried out effectively. It is likely that new photography will be commissioned for some of these areas and this will most likely be in colour or in false colour infra red similar to that available for Exmoor. (See pages 18-19, 22-23, 30, 114-115 and 119).

There is little doubt that aerial photography will continue to play an important role in the identification of historic and archaeological sites and their associated landscapes. Improvements in computerised mapping and picture storage will make it possible to use aerial photographs for a wide variety of development, conservation and educational purposes.

THE FUTURE OF AERIAL PHOTOGRAPHY IN SOMERSET

It is therefore essential that aerial photographs continue to be taken to provide a tool for studying landscape changes and understanding the county. Each flight provides new information and the RCHME, in particular, has agreed to continue to support a programme of work. In addition Somerset County Council, other local authorities and Government bodies have continued to support new aerial photography. The main set of photographs purchased in 1993 was a complete set of colour vertical air photographs of the county taken during 1992. This collection will continue the sequence of photographs which show how the county has developed. These photographs are available for reference and further details are given on page 120.

Aerial photographs are also being increasingly used by many private individuals and public bodies to illustrate a variety of projects, landscapes and developments. Some of this material is being deposited in public archives in the form of reports used for planning applications and major developments, but a considerable amount of new photography is hidden away in private archives. Somerset County Council Sites and Monuments Record in conjunction with the County Archives and Record Service is always interested in obtaining copies of any aerial photographs, especially those which are no longer required for particular projects or reports. This material will then be examined for any archaeological or historic information and the photographs will be stored for public consultation.

The photographs in this book represent more than fifty years of aerial photography in Somerset. Provided that we continue the reconnaissance programme of collecting new photography we will document the heritage of the county for this and subsequent generations.

Chapter 1
The COAST

Somerset is fortunate in having a very varied coastline which ranges from the high cliffs of Exmoor down to the estuarine marshes of Bridgwater Bay. Aerial photographs can be very useful in looking at these areas which are frequently difficult to visit on the ground. This is particularly true of the intertidal areas of Bridgwater Bay where the lines of earlier coastal defences or early silted drainage channels are often visible from the air. The area of sand dunes at Brean and Berrow has gradually been affected by modern developments and caravan parks. Coastal erosion is occurring in the area to the west of Watchet and aerial photographs can be used to record the changing coastline over a period of years.

The small coastal village of **PORLOCK** is the most westerly harbour along the Somerset coast. Porlock is a Saxon name and is thought to refer to the 'enclosure by the harbour'. It is possible that the harbour or bay at Porlock may well have been one of the reasons why the Danes landed here in 918AD. The photograph clearly shows how the village is focused around the church of St Dubricius. The street pattern has not changed since the medieval period and the village contains examples of typical West Somerset buildings dating from the late medieval period through to the nineteenth century.

Today Porlock is an important tourist centre and the picturesque hills along the coast and southwards towards Exmoor attract thousands of visitors each year.
The harbour at **PORLOCK WEIR** is still in regular use for small fishing and pleasure craft.

This oblique view shows the coast between Watchet and Minehead. All along this coast there are small harbours and inlets which were formerly used for coastal trading. Off the coast, fish weirs have been maintained since the early Middle Ages providing fish for local consumption. **BLUE ANCHOR**, named after a public house, began to develop as one of a number of holiday resorts along this coast. Limited permanent building has occurred here but seasonal occupation in caravan parks provides a substantial input to the local economy at various sites along the West Somerset coast.

The resort of **BURNHAM-ON-SEA** developed as a result of the arrival of the Somerset and Dorset railway line in 1858 and the link with Poole in 1863. There was a grand and ambitious idea to link France with Wales using rail and ferries and the port at Burnham-on-Sea. Due to a number of problems the French link never developed and Burnham remained a small seaside resort chiefly serving Somerset and Dorset. This photograph, taken in 1967, shows the sea front and the large concrete pool formed to capture the sea after each high tide. At this time the sea front was liable to occasional flooding which became particularly serious in 1981 when the town was badly flooded. Consequently a large concrete sea wall has been built to protect the town (completed in 1985). In the top left hand corner of the photograph the white tower of the Burnham-on-Sea High Lighthouse is visible. This dates from the middle of the nineteenth century. Much of the housing in the centre of the photograph dates from the expansion of the town brought about by the coming of the railway.

MINEHEAD NORTH HILL. This area contains the evidence of a wide range of earlier activity on the hill. Earliest activity dates back to the Prehistoric period with several Bronze Age barrows and an enclosure. Most of these sites were abandoned for various economic or tenurial reasons and today only one post-medieval farm survives. Since the Second World War the area has also been used for military training and much evidence of this is visible on the ground.

During the dry summers of 1989 and 1990 this area of Minehead suffered from several bad fires which caused considerable damage to the vegetation on the hill. It is clear from this photograph where the rough grazing land and the invasive shrub species survive. This area will require careful management over the next few years if the vegetation is to be re-established in line with current conservation requirements.

An oblique photograph showing the prehistoric enclosure near Furzebury Brake in more detail.

North

On the southern side of **BREAN DOWN** is an extensive sandcliff which was formed as sand and soil was weathered down off the hill and blown up against it. This build up of soil and sand has preserved earlier landscapes which date back to the Palaeolithic period. Archaeological excavation carried out in recent years has shown how this part of Brean Down has been used and occupied. Evidence of a Bronze Age settlement, buildings and a post-Roman cemetery has been found extending over a large area on the south side of the hill in the direction of the existing modern buildings. Coastal erosion has destroyed part of the sandcliff and English Heritage and the National Trust have attempted to prevent further erosion of the cliff by constructing a breakwater of large boulders. The top right photograph shows excavations underway in 1989.

The two main photographs of **BREAN** show how this part of the coast has changed from 1946 to 1992. Gradual development of the caravan parks and recreation facilities have removed some of the sand dunes, although several ecologically important areas still survive today. This narrow neck of land receives thousands of visitors every year.

Chapter 2
SOMERSET UPLANDS

There are five main areas of Somerset which can be classed as upland. In the north, there are the Mendip Hills with their limestone outcrops and drystone walls.

In the western part of the county the Quantock and Brendon Hills each have a distinctive character with open common land on the Quantocks and large areas of pasture over much of the Brendons.

On the borders with Devon the higher parts of Exmoor rise to 443m at Dunkery Beacon. This is also an area which has a distinctive landscape of commons and open grazing with a vegetation of heather and gorse. Exmoor was designated a National Park in 1954 and with increasing Government support through the Environmentally Sensitive Area (ESA) initiative, it will be farmed with conservation firmly in mind.

To the south west of the county the Blackdown Hills stretch into Devon and this is an area which has received little attention until very recently when it was designated an Area of Outstanding Natural Beauty (AONB) and an ESA. It is a landscape which has a particularly good layer of medieval and post medieval activity visible from the air. In a recent survey of the Blackdown Hills 75 sites were identified from aerial photographs which had not been previously noted on the ground.

The Blackdown Hills showing the Wellington Monument erected in 1852.

This photograph shows one of a number of deserted medieval farmsteads on the edge of the Mendips above Wells, Westbury-sub-Mendip and Cheddar known as **RAMSPITS**. As well as the nineteenth century building in its enclosure with a sheep dip there are slighter earthworks of medieval farmhouses, trackways and field banks. The farm was certainly occupied by the early fourteenth century, but seems to have been abandoned in the fifteenth century when we know that the land was leased as pasture. Such farms could either have originated as early medieval sites established by colonists from Westbury working out beyond the common fields of the village, or they might be much older than the villages and the fields representing places established in later prehistoric times.

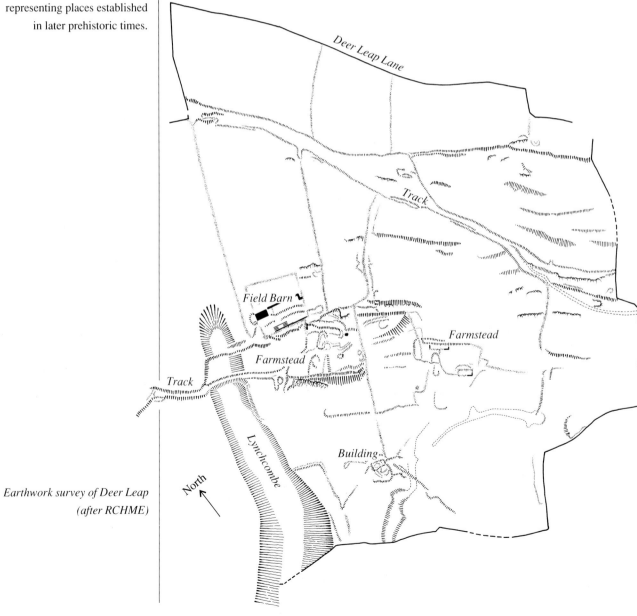

Earthwork survey of Deer Leap (after RCHME)

The landscape of the **QUANTOCK HILLS** has been recognised as a special place for many years, and was designated as the first Area of Outstanding Natural Beauty in England in 1947. In this photograph the upper moorland and heath landscape gives way to the cultivated farmland with its hedges and buildings. At the top of the photograph the undulating hills descend to the coast and further enclosed land to the north. The Quantock Hills AONB is managed by Somerset County Council working in conjunction with a large number of private owners.

The close-up photograph clearly shows the earthwork bank and deep ditch which forms the enclosure known as **TRENDLE RING**. The name Trendle comes from the Old English name for a ring or circle, a good description of this earthwork. There is a large number of similar sites in Somerset and they are usually thought to be of later prehistoric date and indicate a defended enclosure probably around a farm site. Archaeological excavations in other parts of the country have shown that within such enclosures a variety of structures was built, some used as houses and others for stock or agricultural purposes. It is possible that the open, higher land of the Quantocks was used as common grazing land during the Iron Age and enclosures such as Trendle Ring could have been used for the herding and trading of stock, perhaps on a seasonal basis.

This photograph of **WINSFORD HILL** shows how topographical and vegetational characteristics can be examined by the use of 'false colour' images of the countryside. The area is known as *Wambarrow* which is probably the 'Wamburg' mentioned in the perambulation of the Exmoor Forest in 1219 when it was a royal hunting area. There are several barrows visible on this photograph, the most obvious example on the right hand side of the photograph above the main road. There is little doubt that this was a special area in prehistoric times and more recently folklore and legends have grown up which refer to a Black Dog that is reported to be guarding treasure in this part of Winsford Hill.

The line of the road from Dulverton to Simonsbath can be picked out as a thin blue line running across the photograph. Improved grassland shows up as the dark red colour. The area of green land represents the open unimproved common which is partly covered with heather (the darker green areas) and rough grazing (light green). Such areas require careful management and control of the vegetation if the heather is to be encouraged. The designation of Exmoor as an Environmentally Sensitive Area will bring in additional funding to enable the appropriate conservation and management of important areas such as Winsford Hill.

Chapter 3
The MENDIP HILLS

The Mendip Hills stretch for more than 40 kilometres across the northern part of Somerset. The limestone hills have many aspects and aerial photography is particularly good at recording both the natural and man-made parts of the landscape. Cheddar Gorge is one of the most visited parts of the county with more than a million visitors each year looking at the Gorge and its caves. On the top of Mendip are numerous natural features including the swallet holes and cave entrances which have made the Mendips famous for generations of cavers and walkers.

The prehistoric legacy of Somerset is more obvious on Mendip than in any other part of the county. Prehistoric barrows are a common feature visible on almost every ridge across the central part of the hills. Many of these earthworks were investigated in the last century and have been shown to be 3000 years old or more, dating from the Bronze Age. The Romans also left their mark on this landscape particularly by their mining activities extracting lead and silver. Lead from the Mendips has been found at Pompeii arriving there before 79AD when Vesuvius erupted.

In Medieval times the Mendip Hills were owned by the Crown, the Bishops of Bath and Wells and various monastic houses who turned large areas over to sheep farming. The famous Priddy sheep fair continues this tradition of sheep farming on Mendip.

Mendip villages are usually situated at the foot of the hills and this is the picture for the central part of the Hills with such places as Rodney Stoke and Westbury-sub-Mendip. At the eastern end, towards Frome, the settlement pattern changes to more regularly spaced villages as the plateau of the hill becomes less marked. Many of the towns and villages in the Mendip area developed into thriving woollen textile centres from the late medieval period onwards.

The top of the Mendip Hills is rich in prehistoric monuments of Bronze Age date. **PRIDDY NINE BARROWS** can be clearly seen as shadows with a winter sun shining from the left side of this photograph. Within the surrounding fields there are other earthworks some of which are swallet holes and others are associated with lead or other mineral working. Traces of modern field drainage are clearly visible as parallel scored lines on the right hand side of the barrows. Excavations have taken place in several of these barrows revealing cremations often with grave goods such as beads of amber or jet or even bronze daggers. Careful examination of the photograph shows a small group of people looking at the barrows.

CHEDDAR GORGE must be one of the most famous sites in the county receiving visitors almost the whole year round to see the magnificent Gorge and exciting cave systems which trace the story of Somerset folk who have used this area for over 12000 years. The main photograph was taken in the mid 1960s and shows that the sides and edges of the gorge were covered in scrub and small trees. Recently the National Trust and the Longleat Estate have been actively involved in clearing over-hanging and dangerous scrub and other vegetation from the limestone cliff edges.

Visitor pressure and traffic within the Gorge have been major causes of concern in recent years. There is clearly a need to manage visitors more effectively in order that the natural beauty of the Gorge is not lost to the motor car. There will no doubt be continued discussion on this very difficult problem for many years to come.

One of the pioneers of landscape history, W.G. Hoskins, described the English landscape as a palimpsest composed of many layers of activity. This photograph of **CHARTERHOUSE** illustrates this idea very well.

The modern straight lines of the enclosure roads and hedges divide up the landscape into rectangular blocks and a nineteenth century covert or small woodland has been planted in the corner of one of the fields. In the central foreground the surface of the field has been deeply scarred by mining leaving irregular circular holes. This is a landscape which contains a variety of metal ores, and both lead and silver have been worked in this area from Roman times until the present century.

At the top of the photograph the uneven landscape is largely the result of nineteenth century reworking of earlier spoil heaps, particularly for lead. Some of the more subtle features on this photograph are the ploughed-out remains of earthworks. The upper part of the photograph shows a rectangular shape of a Roman camp or military site, presumably a fort. The Romans invaded Britain in AD 43 and within a few years lead was being exported all over the Empire from Charterhouse. The lead and silver mines of the Mendips were one of the important factors which encouraged the Romans to invade Britain.

In the fields below the main road a series of ploughed down banks and ditches which form enclosures can be clearly seen in the winter sunlight. This is an extensive archaeological landscape and one which is in need of careful conservation and management.

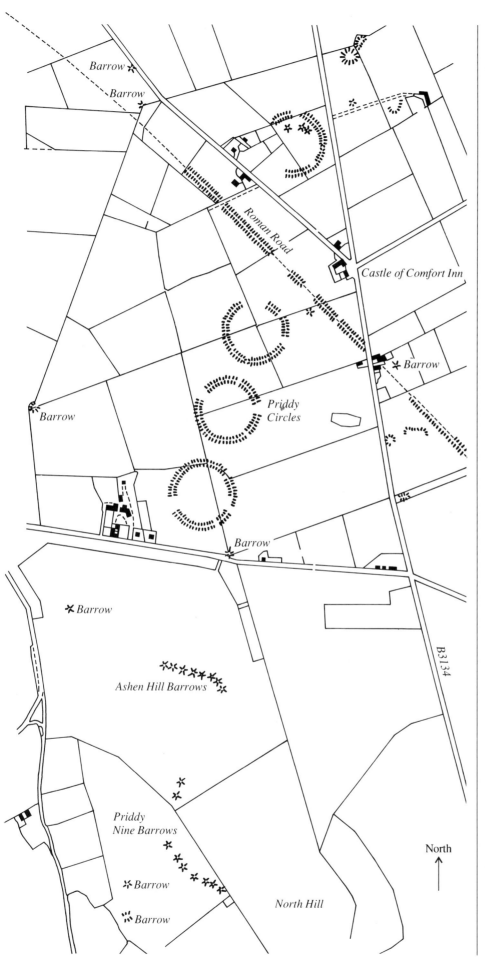

Of all the prehistoric earthwork sites on Mendip the enigmatic **PRIDDY CIRCLES** must be one of the most intriguing to see from the air. It is a landscape which can only really be appreciated from above and consists of three circles which are relatively close together and a fourth circle, which is incomplete, just visible at the top of the photograph.

The purpose and function of these earthworks have not been fully explained but they are often thought to represent some religious or ceremonial centre on the top of Mendip. The association of these circles with the extensive barrow cemeteries close by suggests that this part of Somerset formed a focus similar to those around Stonehenge and Avebury in Wiltshire. Structures of this type are usually thought to date from the late Neolithic or Early Bronze Age period approximately 4000 years ago.

The line of the Roman road from the Mendip mines can also be seen crossing the fields at the top of the photograph.

Chapter 4
The SOMERSET LEVELS and MOORS

The Somerset Levels and Moors covers an area of 650 square kilometres and includes parts of south Somerset, the Axe and Brue valleys and all areas up to the Bristol Channel. They are bounded by the Mendip Hills to the north, the Quantocks to the west and the Blackdown Hills to the south. It is a landscape with dark and deep ditches (rhynes) which have been cut into the peat, and open areas of flat grassland which are edged by wet ditches and pollarded willows.

Six thousand years ago this part of the county was under water for a substantial part of the year. The area gradually became silted up and was no longer subject to inundation from the sea. A freshwater bog produced extensive and deep deposits of peat which probably continued to grow into Saxon times. These deposits have been exploited as a source of fuel since at least the medieval period when they are recorded as part of the turbary lands of the Bishops of Bath and Wells and Glastonbury Abbey. It is within this peat that evidence of early buried trackways and settlements is preserved. Aerial photography is of limited value to monitor archaeological remains buried in the

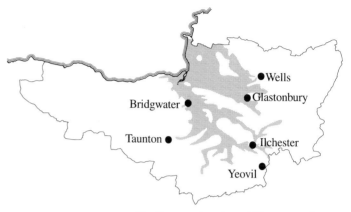

The Somerset Levels and Moors area is indicated by the shading on this map.

peat but it is particularly good at showing the extent of current and old areas of peat working. Recently the commercial extraction of peat for horticultural purposes has caused the widespread destruction of large areas of the Somerset Peat Moors. This extraction continues today although tighter planning laws and changes in environmental awareness have started to affect the peat industry.

It is the area of the flat clay Levels, the 'clay belt' along the coast with their grazing cattle, which are best suited to aerial photography. In some instances, the subtle earthworks which frequently stretch for several kilometres, have their origins in the Roman period although the dating of many of the features visible from aerial photographs is impossible without detailed archaeological investigation. Much research remains to be done on this special part of Somerset.

The long term management of parts of the Somerset Levels and Moors as an Environmentally Sensitive Area will attempt to ensure that it is farmed in a traditional manner. Aerial photographs will be one of the main tools used by the Ministry of Agriculture, Fisheries and Food to monitor changes in this important landscape. The potential of this area for recreation and tourism following water based themes is currently being investigated. There is little doubt that the richness and character of this special landscape, with its wildlife and man-made heritage, will continue to attract more visitors each year. This is one part of the county where 'green tourism' is likely to expand in the next century.

BURROW MUMP is a natural mound in the Levels and its prominence has attracted the attention of people from early times. The oval mound on the top is now thought to be man-made, probably of Norman date, which would have supported a timber look-out tower. The present church was begun in 1793 but insufficient funds were raised to complete it. Burrow Mump is often linked with Alfred in his campaign against the Danes. There is little evidence for this, but Alfred's base at Athelney was only two kilometres away. The River Parrett at the base of the Mump leads into the heart of Somerset and so the Mump would always have had some strategic significance. Burrow Mump was given to the National Trust as Somerset's memorial to those who fell in the Second World War.

Alfred's Monument, Athelney (erected in 1801) with Burrow Mump visible in the background, painted by Harry Frier c.1880

This picture shows one of the most famous landmarks in Somerset. The natural hill of
GLASTONBURY TOR is terraced all around and crowned by a medieval stone tower, all
that is left of the church of St Michael. The terraces are probably strip lynchets of medieval
cultivation although it has also been claimed, fancifully, that the terraces represent a maze.
Excavations on the summit showed that the hill top had been occupied in prehistoric times.
There may have been an Iron Age and Roman temple and there seems to have been a
monastic, or more likely, a hermitage settlement in the 'Dark Ages'. Much of the earlier
evidence was removed when a platform was constructed for the Norman Church. The hill
continues to act as a focus for visitors every year.

Throughout the Somerset Levels and Moors are numerous features which are connected with water management and with wildlife. The earliest references to decoy pools in England occur in the medieval period but the majority of pools originated in the seventeenth or eighteenth centuries. The decoys were used to trap wildfowl in a variety of different ways. The most common type, like this example at **GODNEY**, originated in Holland and was brought over to England during the seventeenth century by Dutch experts. It is interesting that at this same period the drainage of the Somerset Levels and Moors was going through a very active phase. The natural pools and ponds, such as Meare Pool, were drained by the end of the seventeenth century and were no longer available for local landowners to use as a wildfowl larder. It was therefore necessary to construct artificial pools. The nineteenth century expert on duck decoys, Payne Gallwey, recommended pools should be between 1 and 2 acres in extent (0.4 -0.8ha) with a depth of not more than 3 feet (1m).

Radiating outwards from the pond, gradually reducing in size, were long thin arms called pipes. A net was stretched over these pipes and the ducks, usually mallard, teal and widgeon were trapped in the pipes by a man with a dog. The natural curious ducks follow the dog which lead to their captured. Decoy pools provided landowners with a steady income and in the seventeenth and eighteenth centuries many pools made a profit from the sale of birds. They did, however, require a sizeable investment; a pool at Compton Dundon was constructed in 1695 and cost £135 9s $2^1/_2$d. With the development of duck shooting as a sport in the later part of the nineteenth century, many decoys went out of use and became silted up suriving now only as earthworks. A recent survey of the Somerset Levels and Moors has shown that 45 decoy sites survive in Somerset. Duck decoys which are still worked in the traditional way can be seen at Slimbridge in Gloucestershire and Boarstall in Buckinghamshire.

A nineteenth century illustration of a decoy man driving a duck up a pipe. From 'The Book of Duck Decoys' by Payne-Gallwey (1886)

Many attempts were made to control the flooding problems of the Brue Valley but it was not until the construction of the **HUNTSPILL RIVER** that water was controlled here. It runs for more than 8km westward to the Severn Estuary draining much of the Brue valley. It cuts across the field boundaries and rhynes (drainage ditches) of the largely eighteenth century drained landscape demonstrating that it is a modern feature. It was constructed during the Second World War to provide water for the Royal Ordnance Factory at Puriton, near Bridgwater.

SOMERSET PEAT has been excavated as a source of fuel for hundreds of years but it is only since the 1950s that large-scale commercial peat digging has removed such extensive tracts of the Somerset landscape. The alternating pattern of dark and light stripes of peat cuts in grass fields leaves a characteristic 'zebra' pattern. After cutting, the peat is stacked and dried in the fields and then brought into the factories for processing and packaging for the commercial market.

The future of peat extraction both in Somerset and nationally is the subject of considerable environmental debate. Appropriate conservation and management of such landscapes requires cooperation if such areas are to be passed on to subsequent generations.

Peatworks and peatfields near Meare

Few motorists on the M5 motorway can have failed to notice the hill and hillfort at **BRENT KNOLL**. This view shows how the hill rises from the surrounding floodlands of the Axe valley. The top of the hill has been moulded and shaped by many centuries of activity. The earthworks are thought to date from the Iron Age and observations by the Rev. John Skinner, the great early Somerset antiquary (1772-1839), recorded Roman and Iron Age objects from the hill. There is little doubt that it was an important strategic and military site for many years. It was last defended during the Second World War and a number of slit trenches were cut by the Home Guard, particularly on the eastern side. The irregular mounds and hollows within the upper part of the earth-work were produced by quarrying, and almost half the hilltop has been affected in this way. The hill is surrounded by a number of gently curving hedges which radiate from it following natural contours of the land. Evidence of drainage ditches and curving (medieval) field strip lynchets are clearly visible in the upper right hand part of the photograph.

This is a good example of a shadow photograph, characterised by the long shadows of the bare trees.

Chapter 5
ARCHAEOLOGICAL SITES

Archaeological sites survive in a wide range of sizes, shapes and periods. The earliest are the caves of the first people to come to Somerset over half a million years ago. Later periods of prehistory are characterised by burial mounds, ritual earthworks and defended settlements. During Roman, Saxon and early medieval times the basic settlement and land use pattern was established which we can still see today. The photographs selected in this chapter show a number of the well known sites within Somerset such as Ham Hill and South Cadbury Castle. It also includes some of the newly discovered sites such as the cropmark sites at Chedzoy and Stanchester. Aerial photography is particularly useful to archaeologists and historians to enable investigation and recording of landscapes which are often difficult to get to, or do not show evidence at ground level. The examples given here show the quality and diversity of evidence which makes up the archaeological heritage of Somerset. There are approximately ten thousand archaeological sites known within Somerset and several thousand of these have been identified from aerial photographs. The existence of a whole buried landscape can appear for a very short time depending on many factors such as weather conditions and the vigilance of the aerial photographer. Regular reconnaissance is essential in productive areas.

The very name **STANCHESTER** has a distinctive archaeological association deriving from the old English *stane* (stone) and *ceastra* meaning 'camp', a word often used by the Saxons for earlier Roman sites. No Roman finds have yet been made in this area however, and the main features visible are almost certainly much older. Small circular cropmarks are not uncommon in Somerset and are usually interpreted as the ditches of ploughed-out barrows, but features as large as this are rare. It is possible this site is a henge-type monument, like Priddy Circles, of late Neolithic or early Bronze Age date. The smaller, sub-rectangular enclosure also visible could be the site of a small Romano-British farmstead which gave the site its name.

This photograph, taken in the dry summer of 1990, shows a wide range of earlier ditches, boundaries, pits and enclosures in the **CHEDZOY** area. Towards the top, a rectangular ditched enclosure with a break for an entrance is visible. Features of this type are usually thought to date from the Romano-British period and are probably agricultural settlements. A regular grid pattern of long rectangular fields can be seen in the centre. On the left of the modern road the most obvious feature is a long U-shaped enclosure which may have continued into the field below it. Crop-marks of this size and shape are uncommon in Somerset and it may represent the ploughed-out remains of a ditched enclosure of Neolithic or Early Bronze Age date known as a *cursus*. The function of such enclosures is open to debate but they are usually interpreted as having a ceremonial or religious function. No other examples are currently known in Somerset.

The series of regular polygonal marks which occur across the photograph are natural features produced in the Ice Age as a result of 'freeze-thaw' action of the ground. A number of small squarish 'blobs' on the left of the photograph represent pits of unknown date but may suggest possible Saxon settlement remains.

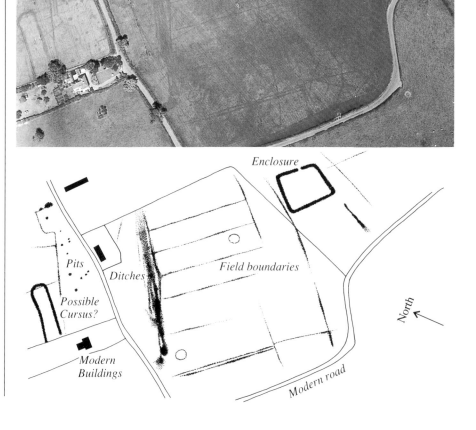

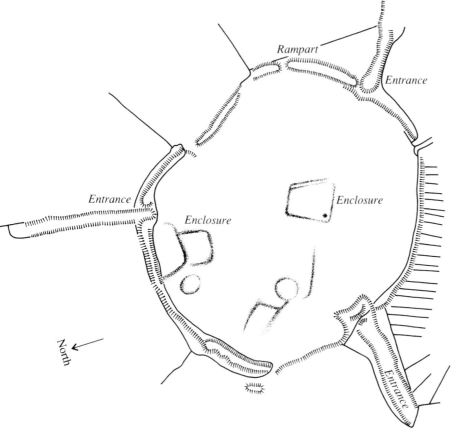

Rampart

Entrance

Entrance

Enclosure

Enclosure

Entrance

North

Situated west of Taunton, the prehistoric hillfort at **NORTON FITZWARREN** is rarely visited by anyone other than local people following the circular walk which runs around the inner part of the ramparts. The ramparts enclose an area of approximately $5\frac{1}{2}$ hectares and the whole interior has been ploughed for many years. When viewed from the air the positions of numerous rectangular ditches, smaller enclosures and other features can be seen as differential crop growth in a field of ripening corn. Excavations at Norton Fitzwarren in 1908 and in the early 1970s have shown that the site was occupied in the Mesolithic (6000BC) and Neolithic (4000BC) periods, and by the Bronze Age c.2000 BC an enclosure had been constructed here. The site continued to be occupied in the Iron Age when the substantial ditches, ramparts and entrances were constructed. The rectangular enclosures visible on this photograph are likely to date from the Roman period and fieldwalking of the site in 1991 produced Roman pottery. It is not clear if the site was occupied in the post Roman period as so many hillforts were in Somerset. A local legend suggests that it may have been, and that it was formerly remembered as the main centre of Taunton.

*"Norton was a market town
when Taunton was a furzy down"*

*Romano-British pottery finds from
Norton Fitzwarren Hillfort*

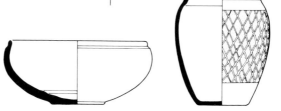

CADBURY CASTLE is not a 'castle' in the medieval sense but a prehistoric hillfort defended by lines of banks and ditches. These can be seen to the left of the hill (south and south-east sides) but are otherwise obscured by the woodland. The defences were constructed in the Iron Age period 2300 years ago when the hilltop would have been full of round houses. It was also occupied in the Roman period when there may have been a temple here. It was later refortified and formed the base of a war leader, who some would identify as King Arthur. In the early eleventh century there seems to have been an abortive attempt to develop a fortified hill top town on this site when a church was laid out, coins minted and the defences refurbished. An extensive programme of archaeological excavations was undertaken in the 1960s and 1970s, and a full publication of these excavations will soon be produced by English Heritage. The excavations at South Cadbury have shown the significance of this site over several thousand years.

Situated in the eastern part of the Mendip Hills, the Iron Age hillfort of **MAESBURY CASTLE** is visible on the right-hand side of the photograph. It is one of the best preserved examples in this part of Somerset. The rampart is more than six metres high in places and careful stock grazing has ensured good grass cover, helping to prevent erosion of the bank, ditch and entrance earthworks. There has been limited archaeological investigation of the site and little is known of what there was of occupation or structures in its interior. When viewed from the air, Maesbury is visible as the only circular feature in a sea of largely straight lines of enclosure walls and hedges. The field pattern dates from the enclosure of the area in the late eighteenth and early nineteenth centuries. The Roman road along the Mendips can be seen as a low linear earthwork from the bottom left to the centre top of the photograph. Part of the curving disused railway line from Shepton Mallet to Radstock crosses the photograph. Abandoned railway cuttings of this type can be particularly beneficial to the ecology and natural history of an area and it is becoming increasingly common practice to protect such sites and areas from tipping or infilling.

Few travellers moving rapidly through the southern part of Somerset on the recently constructed A303 will be aware that they are driving past one of the largest Iron Age hillforts in Britain. The archaeological story of the occupation on **HAM HILL** is very complex and can be traced back into the Neolithic and Bronze Age periods almost 4000 years ago. Excavations and chance finds have shown that there was very extensive occupation here in the Iron Age. Evidence of considerable Roman activity, both military in the form of armour, and domestic in the form of a Roman villa, has been found within the hillfort. The natural outcrop of Jurassic limestone which forms the hill above the village of Stoke sub Hamdon has also been quarried since the Roman period for its distinctive honey-coloured building stone. The quarrying activity continues to the present day and was particularly extensive in the early years of the present century when a small railway system was in operation within the quarrying areas at this northern end of the

hillfort. The pitted ground with its system of tracks and spoil heaps has left a strange and unusual landscape. This end of the hillfort is currently managed as a Country Park. The top photograph clearly shows the ramparts at the northern end of the hillfort before they were so overgrown with invasive scrub and trees. This photograph was taken before the hillfort was a Country Park and there was substantially less visitor erosion of the ramparts or of the interior of the hillfort. Current efforts to manage and interpret the hillfort will help in the long-term protection of this important part of our heritage so that it can be appreciated and enjoyed.

King Alfred is known to have visited Cheddar, and there are records of a palace here used by the late Saxon and early medieval kings - Edmund, William I (The Conqueror) and II, Henry I and II and John. Before the **KINGS OF WESSEX SCHOOL**, shown here, was built in the 1960s a large scale excavation by Philip Rahtz located the outlines of the timber buildings used by the kings, next to the surviving stone chapel of St Columbanus (centre of picture). The sites of these buildings are marked out with concrete posts (centre) and show the tenth century hall (left) where Edmund negotiated with St Dunstan over Glastonbury Abbey in 940AD and the great aisled hall of Henry I and II (twelfth century) to the right.

Below is a reconstruction drawing of the complex by the late Alan Sorrell.

This photograph shows the earthworks which survive in the area around the Roman **Fort** at **CHARTERHOUSE**. The rectangular shape of the fort with its outer banks and ditches has been damaged by ploughing and the earthwork has been much reduced in size. Nevertheless, this earthwork is a rare survival in south west England, an area with few Roman forts. In the foreground are the undulating remains of the former lead mining spoil heaps and tipping areas of the nineteenth century. In the top right hand corner are more earthworks of probable Roman date.

Roman remains have been noted in the area of **FOSSE LANE, SHEPTON MALLET** since the construction of the Shepton to Wincanton railway line in 1867. It was not, however, until 1989 that a large scale, detailed archaeological excavation of the site was undertaken in advance of redevelopment of the site for housing and industrial use. The excavation revealed the extensive remains of buildings, yards, roads, trackways and, more importantly, a late Roman cemetery with Christian associations. This site should be seen as a linear 'village' or small roadside town and only fifty similar sites are known in England.

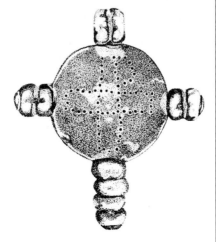

The most unusual artefact from the site is a silver alloy cross with an punched Chi-Ro monogram (the first two letters of 'Christ' in Greek) on a central disc found with a burial. These symbols indicate that a Christian community existed at Shepton Mallet in the fifth century.

Chapter 6
FIELDS AND FARMS

The countryside between our towns and villages is dotted with farms and farmsteads. In the eastern and southern part of Somerset many of the farms are to be found within or adjacent to the main villages. The pattern in the western and higher parts of the county shows farms scattered or dispersed across wider areas. The arable and pasture lands which were worked by these farms have been moulded into characteristic field shapes frequently with large and distinctive boundaries of hedges planted on banks.

The effects of more than six thousand years of farming on the countryside can frequently be seen from the air. In some areas, particularly on the higher lands of Exmoor or the Mendip Hills, evidence of former field systems can be clearly seen. Some of these field systems date from the prehistoric or medieval periods when climatic conditions were better than they are today.

Today, parts of Somerset are farmed in a very intensive manner and the effects of modern ploughing, drainage and hedgerow removal have virtually destroyed the standing remains of the old landscapes. However, it is in these areas that modern agricultural methods have revealed the crop and soil marks of the earlier farms and fields of prehistoric and Roman Somerset.

In Saxon and Medieval times the settlement pattern of many of our existing farms and villages was established. Each settlement would have had its own field system, perhaps a two or three field system in the central and eastern part of the county and a similar 'infield' and 'outfield' system towards Exmoor and the west.

Enclosure of common land took place during the eighteenth and nineteenth centuries and in some instances new farms were established such as Larkbarrow on Exmoor. Agricultural improvements in the nineteenth century saw numerous model farms built around the county and many survived until relatively recently. Within the last few years agricultural changes and revised subsidies have resulted in changes in farming practice. Many traditional farm barns and out-buildings have been converted for residential use because they are no longer needed to support the modern farm.

This vertical photograph shows the fields and farms around Kittisford and Stawley in the western part of the Vale of Taunton. The settlement pattern is characterised by dispersed farmsteads and Devon-like lanes weaving their way through this gently rolling countryside.

North

In the southern and eastern parts of the county **RIDGE AND FURROW** relics of the medieval common field systems survive as earthworks. This photograph, in the parish of West Camel, shows a group of strips coming together in the corner of a field. These were produced by the action of generations of medieval plough teams of oxen moving up and down the fields.

While three open fields are generally thought to have been used in medieval England, in Somerset in the middle ages, two fields were also found. Often these field systems manifest themselves in the ground as ridge and furrow earthworks. There is a close relationship between the strips as a former tenurial unit in the open fields and the ridges on the ground. The ridges would have served both to drain the arable land and to mark each tenant farmer's holding. Such systems of open fields were progressively abandoned, the lands being enclosed and farmed privately by individual owners. At first this was a piecemeal process but in the eighteenth and nineteenth century specific acts of Parliament were passed to enclose particular parishes. This was not common in Somerset as much land had already been enclosed by 1750.

This vertical photograph, taken in 1947, shows the medieval ridge and furrow pattern around Lovington. Many of these strips have now been removed by modern ploughing.

North

The earthworks of the deserted medieval village of **NETHER ADBER** are some of the best of this type of site in the county. A settlement is first recorded in this area as *Eadber* in the Domesday Book of 1086, and the name suggests that the settlement originated in the late Saxon period in an area that had been wooded. A village developed here with its common fields in the early middle ages and was abandoned as a consequence of a change to sheep farming in the fifteenth century. This photograph shows the remains of old trackways, water courses, paddocks and house sites. The earthworks were damaged over thirty years ago but they are now protected. The surrounding fields, which have evidence of ridge and furrow cultivation from the former common fields (the East Field and West Field), have now all been ploughed away. The village site was acquired by Somerset County Council, with aid from English Heritage, in order to prevent further damage and it is now open to the public.

Situated high up on Exmoor about 6km north east of Simonsbath is the deserted farmstead known as **LARKBARROW**. The farm takes its name from a prehistoric barrow which was noted in 1678 as being one of the boundary markers of the Royal Forest of Exmoor. A map of 1676 sketches in a barrow but its exact position is no longer known. This farm, along with other farms such as Warren Farm and Tom's Hill, was built by Sir Frederick Knight, son of the John Knight who had started the reclamation of the Forest of Exmoor around 1820. In spite of extensive efforts Exmoor proved to be a difficult area to tame. Soil improvements were made to enable grass to grow and store cattle could then be fed throughout the winter. Larkbarrow and Tom's Hill Farm were destroyed in World War II when the area was used for military training.

Enclosure of the uplands in Somerset took place mainly in the eighteenth and nineteenth centuries. This resulted in a regular pattern of straight field boundaries with square corners and straight sides. **WILLETT TOWER** on the Brendon Hills, enclosed with stone and turf banks topped with beech hedging, was erected in 1774 following a successful attempt to raise £130 by local subscription. It is 25 metres high and perhaps served as a 'steeple' or landmark for local horsemen.

TWITCHEN DESERTED FARM SITE, OARE. This picture shows a deserted medieval farm site as the sun highlights the earthworks. The farm was still in existence in 1840 when a survey gives details of the farm buildings and the rents due. At that date the building in the centre was a long-house with the family accommodation uphill (to the right) and rooms for the cattle to the north (left).

North

This vertical photograph shows the area around **MONKSILVER** and Nettlecombe Court in the western part of Somerset. An estate called *Silver* existed in this area in Saxon times. Three separate entries for 'Selve' are noted in the Domesday Book of 1086. The estate at Silver was given to the monks at Goldcliffe in 1113 and it was then passed on to Tewkesbury Abbey. Nettlecombe Court is now the Leonard Wills Field Centre and is administered by the Field Studies Council. The present house, standing with its fine landscaped grounds, was originally owned by the Ralegh family and they are likely to have been associated with building a church here in c.1300. Much of the present house and grounds was built by the Trevelyan family who owned this manor from c.1480 through to the present day. This photograph shows how many of the larger fields, particularly near Black Down Wood (top of the photograph) have been ploughed and improved for arable crops. These fields are in marked contrast with the grassland fields associated with the parkland and pasture of Nettlecombe Court.

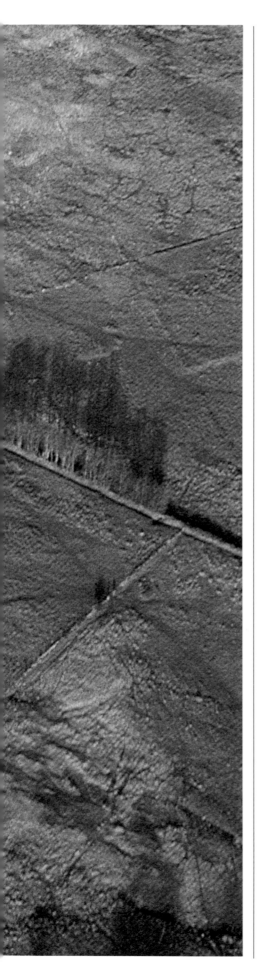

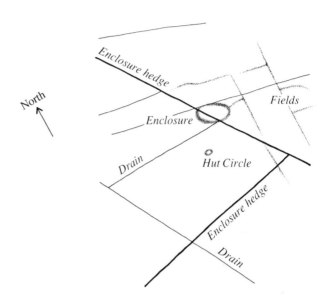

Aerial photographs are particularly useful for looking at the wide open moorland landscape of Exmoor. Providing that the photographs are taken in the right conditions it is possible to see a wide range of earlier field systems on the moor. Some of these date from the prehistoric period and are characterised by rubble banks and lynchets which here extend for several hundred metres across **CODSEND MOORS** and **KITNOR HEATH**. Other field system features which survive on Exmoor are much more recent and are associated with water meadows and leats. Many of these are post medieval in origin often the work of the Knight family who attempted to improve Exmoor in the first half of the nineteenth century. The straight field boundaries, often topped with beech hedges, usually date from the first half of the nineteenth century.

Chapter 7
TOWNS and VILLAGES

Throughout Somerset there are many examples of historic towns and villages. There are currently 160 Conservation Areas which range from the smaller towns and villages such as Milverton or Buckland St Mary to the centres of historic towns such as Glastonbury or Crewkerne. Within these centres hundreds of historic buildings and familiar street scenes contribute to the character of our towns and villages.

When viewed from the air other aspects of historic settlements are also visible. This is particularly true when considering the plan and shape of towns and villages where regular plots of land, earlier defensive features or road alignments can be traced within the existing street pattern. Good examples of this can be seen in towns such as Wells or Taunton.

Aerial photographs can also be used to record the growth and development of towns and villages in a most graphic way. In particular the vertical photographs taken at ten year intervals will provide a valuable source of historic information for future researchers.

On the southern and western side of **YEOVIL** is the large manufacturing works of the Westland Group, famous for its helicopters. The field in the centre of the photograph is the main testing airfield of the works. This part of Yeovil has recently seen developments in the form of an improved road network and the growth of industrial estates and housing. The development of Yeovil is continuing both to the west and the north sides of the town.

Situated on the southern slopes of the Mendip Hills the small town of **AXBRIDGE** is now bypassed by a modern road constructed along the disused Cheddar Valley Railway Line. There was no early bridge across the River Axe in the area of the town although one may have existed elsewhere. The settlement probably takes its name from the Saxon *burh* or fort, recorded in the tenth century document, the Burghal Hidage, which is thought to have been sited on the southern side of the market place. In such a position a fort would have been well placed to control east-to-west communications in the Axe valley, and to protect the Saxon royal centre at Cheddar of which Axbridge was an appendage, an arrangement recorded in the Domesday Book of 1086. The present church is largely of fifteenth century date and is situated on a ridge of land on the north side of the market place.

The small market town of **BRUTON** takes its name from the River Brue which divides the settlement into two parts. In Saxon times there was a small town and mint at Bruton but no archaeological evidence has so far been noted to identify where the early settlement was. There may have been a monastery here in the tenth century which became a house of Augustinian canons between 1127 and 1135. Building work continued around the monastery in the early part of the sixteenth century but after 1539 the site was sold and built over to form a large mansion. Today much of the Abbey site is part of King's School which has its origins in the early sixteenth century. On the north side of the River Brue the layout of the High Street area suggests that this was a planned settlement of medieval date. This area of the town contains several fine buildings ranging in date from the sixteenth to the eighteenth centuries and Bruton is a particularly good example of a small historic town.

BRIDGWATER seems to have been developed as a speculative venture by William Briwere around 1200. He built a castle, a bridge and laid out a town which was defended by earthen banks, ditches and gates. No doubt the port was also developed as a transhipment point for goods entering and leaving Somerset. Documentary records indicate that the medieval bridge had three arches and was 122 ft long. In 1795 the stone bridge was replaced by a single-span iron bridge, made at Coalbrookdale and one of the earliest iron bridges in England, which was in turn replaced in 1883.

Little trace of Bridgwater castle can be found on the ground today but the street pattern around Fore Street and West Quay (middle left) follows the line of the castle defences. The last surviving parts of the castle were demolished at the beginning of the nineteenth century when the elegant King Square was built.

In the eighteenth and nineteenth centuries Bridgwater developed as a small but productive industrial centre producing bricks, tiles and glass. These products were exported from the town by various means involving the canal and docks (built between 1837 and 1841) and the railway.

Industrial development has continued at Bridgwater and industrial estates and business parks have been developed on the northern and eastern side of the town.

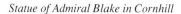

Statue of Admiral Blake in Cornhill

The town of **CHARD** is one of the best examples of a planned medieval borough in Somerset. The original village is thought to have been around the church and manor farm south of the main road from Salisbury to Exeter where there is still a street called 'Old Town'. The main road formed the High Street of the planned town and charters of 1206 and 1234 granted by the Bishop of Bath and Wells give details of the town's limits. The road was laid out as a wide market place almost one kilometre long. Alongside were the town properties or burgages running from the market place street frontage to the rear property line and back lane. The lines of more than fifty of these long thin burgage plots have been identified although in recent times their outlines have been obscured by car parks and other unsympathetic developments. This pattern of properties goes back to the very origins of Chard as a town over seven hundred years ago. They are as important as the earliest documents which have survived.

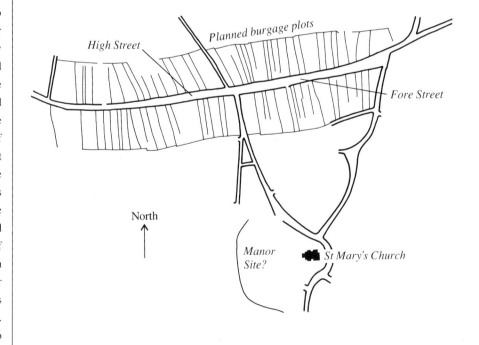

EAST LYNG. This area is famous for its associations with King Alfred and his stay in Somerset prior to routing the Danes in 878AD. It is recorded in the Anglo-Saxon Chronicle that a fort was built at Athelney (west of Lyng) and this was likely to have been constructed on the western end of the main island. A few years later a monastery was established on the island by Alfred and this abbey survived until the Dissolution of the monasteries in 1539. Another Anglo-Saxon document called the Burghal Hidage records that there was a defended area at Lyng with a wall of 412 feet (126m) long. The position of this site has been established at the western end of the village near the church where archaeological evidence of defences have been noted. Lyng was connected to Athelney by a causeway which crossed the wet marsh and an earlier course of the River Tone.

The A361 runs through the middle of the village and most of the houses are built along the road frontage on the higher land. Many of the closes, orchards and paddocks which surround the village are scheduled as an ancient monument.

In the seventeenth and eighteenth centuries **FROME** was one of the largest towns in Somerset
and still contains a large number of very fine buildings of this date. The settlement owes its
origins to a minster which was founded by St Aldhelm (d.709AD), and by 1086 a market was
established here. The town developed between the church and the river with the street pattern
following a long triangular market place. It owed much of its prosperity to the expanding
woollen industry and by c.1660 a large area to the west of the medieval town and the parish
church was developed for housing. This area known as 'Trinity' can be seen still preserved in
the street pattern of the town on the left of centre of this photograph.

The village of **HINTON ST GEORGE** is one of the most 'manufactured' English villages in the county. It is an estate village which was largely built and dominated by the Earls Poulett who lived in Hinton House from the fifteenth through to the present century. The manor house, church and many of the buildings in the village are all of Ham stone. This aerial photograph shows the regular planned nature of the village High Street and the position of the back lane on the south side.

The Roman town of Lendiniae, now called **ILCHESTER**, grew up at the point where the Fosse Way crossed the River Yeo. Originally the site of a fort, the town grew over several hundred years and was larger than the later medieval and modern town. In the 1086 Domesday Book Ilchester was second only to Bath in importance in Somerset with a market, burgages and a mint. The town was the county town for administrative and judicial purposes for over seven hundred years until 1846.

This aerial photograph shows the intersection of the two Roman roads which dominate the town plan and the development of the settlement. Aerial photography is of little use at Ilchester to help to locate archaeological remains in the town because the archaeological deposits are often half a metre or more below the existing ground level. The fields adjacent to the River Yeo contain numerous earthworks some of which are natural water courses and others are likely to be of Roman or medieval date.

The line of the A303 Ilchester By-pass is clearly visible on the left of the photograph.

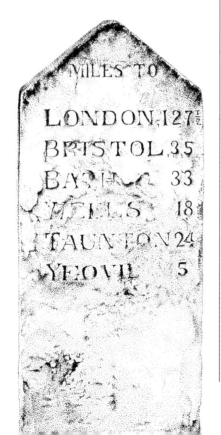

Roman coin   *Saxon coin*

Milestone from Ilchester

The town of **LANGPORT** had its origins in the Anglo Saxon period. It is first noted as a Saxon 'burgh' or fortified place in a document called the Burghal Hidage which is a list of fortified places set up against the Danes in the early tenth century. The original focus for the Saxon fort was centred around the hill in the area of the Church. Remains of earthworks still survive in the area of former St Gildas' Convent fields and archaeological excavations in 1991 revealed pottery of late Saxon date in this area. The rampart of the fort runs across the side of the playing fields below the hill. In the early medieval period burgage plots were laid out running along a causeway towards the bridge over the River Parrett. This causeway has been excavated in places and seems to be of twelfth century date. It was lined with buildings many of which were probably merchants' houses with yards and closes off the river beyond. The layout of burgage plots is still largely intact and this 'planned town' is perhaps the best example of its type in Somerset. The limits of the town are largely dictated by the extent of the flood meadows and with the exception of the warehouses and industrial buildings on the west side of the Parrett, development at Langport has largely been at the eastern end. At the western end two medieval suburbs were developed to cash in on the commercial success of the town. The town contains a number of fine Georgian and Victorian buildings and is also noted for its medieval 'hanging chapel' - so called because it 'hangs' across the road.

The village of **LYMPSHAM** in the north western corner of Somerset is a good example of a scattered village which has no obvious central place in the form of a crossroads or green. Parts of the church date from the fourteenth century although it was largely rebuilt between c.1820 and 1840 by the Stephenson family who were rectors and lords of the manor. The village contains several fine buildings of nineteenth century date. In particular the rectory of 1814-15 is one of the best examples of the romantically gothicized house in Somerset. This photograph, taken before the arrival of Dutch Elm disease, show the wooded nature of the landscape and the field boundaries. In the foreground is good evidence of relatively modern drainage patterns presumably connected with drainage and agricultural improvements at the end of the last century. A number of new houses have been built in the village in recent years but the basic plan and character of the village is still visible today.

Situated in the south east corner of the county the small market town of **MILBORNE PORT** straddles the A30. It is a town with origins in the Saxon period being an important Royal estate. The church contains some of the finest Romanesque architecture in Somerset and was clearly an important minster church in the eleventh century. The road pattern of the medieval town shows a triangular market place, now partly infilled by housing, adjacent to the busy A30.

NORTH CURRY is situated on the edge of the Somerset Levels and Moors and its parish church has often been described as the 'Cathedral of the Somerset Moors'. It is a substantial building dating from the fourteenth century and is set within a roughly oval shaped churchyard. At the southern end of the churchyard, the two edges of the medieval planned green or market place are visible. Nearby are earthworks of ponds, enclosures and platforms which probably mark the medieval manor site.

Somerset has few village greens, and with the stone walls and stone-built houses this view of **PRIDDY** is more reminiscent of Derbyshire or Yorkshire than Somerset. There were few villages and farms on the top of the Mendips but the local water and soil conditions at Priddy always proved useful to people in earlier prehistoric times. In August a sheep fair is held and this dates back to medieval times. On the green is a stack of hurdles, for legend says that if the hurdles should ever disappear so too will Priddy.

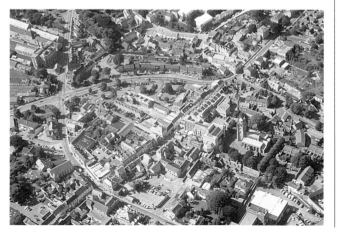

SHEPTON MALLET. At the time of the Domesday Book Shepton or 'Sepetone' (meaning 'sheep town') was held as part of the lands of Glastonbury Abbey. The village was developed by the Abbey and their tenants, the Malet family, as a town with burgages and a weekly market in 1235 and an annual fair in 1318. In the eighteenth and nineteenth centuries the river served as an important focus for development when several silk mills and the large Anglo Bavarian Brewery were built.

The village of **MILVERTON** is situated in the rolling hills on the west side of the Vale of Taunton. Like many in Somerset it has its origins in the Anglo-Saxon period. The place name is usually thought to derive from 'the farm of the mill-ford' and a mill is recorded in Domesday Book of 1086. Its exact position is unknown but it is usually thought to have been situated in the area of the existing mill on the Hillfarrance Brook which can be seen to the north (top) of the village. It is likely that the main Saxon part of the settlement was centred along High Street and around the church of St Michael on the hilltop in the middle of the village. A circular street pattern around the church and the hilltop can be clearly seen from the air. Milverton contains several impressive late medieval and eighteenth century buildings and developed as a wealthy satellite village of Taunton long before the railway arrived. The modern bypass runs along the old railway line (top of photograph).

North

SOMERTON was an important royal estate in the Anglo-Saxon period and there may have been a palace here. However the earliest features that can be seen on this air photograph relate to the planning of a new medieval town in the thirteenth century. This had a grid plan with the main streets, Broad Street and West Street, at right angles to each other with a large rectangular market place in between. Somerton housed the county gaol and court between 1278 and 1371 and it is this function which probably caused the town to be known as 'an ancient capital town'. The market cross and Market House remain to show the original function of this open space. The medieval pattern of long thin burgage properties can be seen along every street.

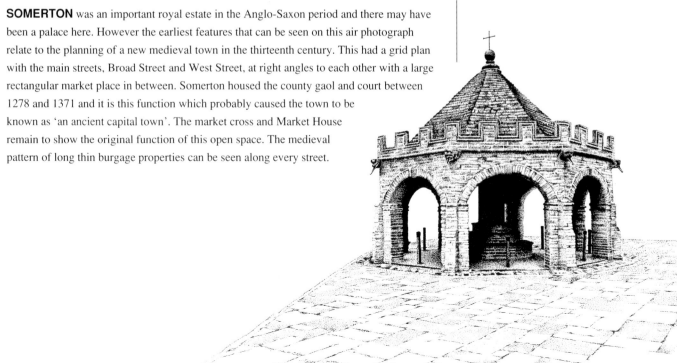

The town of **STREET** takes its name from a Roman road which ran to the east of the town. There is little doubt that the early village was situated in the area of the parish church. The church was at one time dedicated to St Gildas but it is currently dedicated to the Holy Trinity. The regular street pattern of nineteenth century industrial housing is evident from this aerial photograph. It shows neat rows of houses and small gardens which were part of the planned development funded by the Clarks - a strong Quaker family who invested in their community. Street was chosen as the headquarters of the shoe company which was established here in 1825 initially to produce sheepskin rugs and slippers. By the middle of the last century Clarks had expanded considerably and by the end the population of the town had grown to almost 4000. Today the town continues to provide employment for many people from Glastonbury and the central Somerset area.

This oblique view shows the central part of the historic core of medieval **TAUNTON**. Although it is referred to in the Anglo-Saxon period there is no clear evidence, either historical or archaeological, of a town at Taunton before Domesday Book in 1086 which mentions burgages, a market and a mint (for producing coins). By the twelfth century the town had an 'embankment' with a ditch for defence. At the bottom of the photograph is the area of Taunton Castle, now the County Museum and headquarters of the Somerset Archaeological and Natural History Society. In the centre of the photograph the triangle of roads formed a market place, now dominated by the Market House, built in 1772. The church towers of St Mary Magdalene (left) and St George (top) dominate the rooflines of the town. Modern developments, particularly in the top left of the photograph, have destroyed much of the medieval street and property pattern which survived until c.1970. Today Taunton is the county town of Somerset, an expanding market town serving a wide catchment area for shopping, services and local government.

The settlement of **WEDMORE** is one of the main centres of population in the middle of the Levels and Moors. There is archaeological evidence of Roman settlement on this island site and recent excavations have shown that there was a settlement here in the late Saxon period. Wedmore is identified in the Anglo Saxon Chronicle and it is noted that in 878AD Guthrum, the newly baptised Danish king, accepted Christianity at Aller and confirmed this at the so-called 'Peace of Wedmore' ceremony. The church of St Mary dominates the street scene, situated on a natural hill in the middle of the village but there is no suggestion from the fabric of the building that an early Anglo Saxon church existed here. Wedmore never really developed into a true medieval town although the place name of *The Borough* still survives today. A regular pattern of field drainage ditches can be seen surrounding the 'island' of buildings.

The plan of **WELLINGTON** is dominated by the long main street, the A38 road to Exeter. The medieval church of St John the Baptist is at the eastern end of the town and buildings of the town stretch for almost 1km westwards. This regular plan of burgages on each side of the road is indicative of medieval town planning. The estate at Wellington was held by the Bishop of Bath and Wells and it has been suggested that during the twelfth and thirteenth centuries the 'new town' was established as a speculative venture by the Bishop.

The aerial photograph shows how the town is crossed by a north to south road which met in the area of the former market place where the High Street widened out. The boundary lines of the medieval burgage plots can be seen running back from both the High Street and Fore Street.

The development of Wellington can be compared with the planned development of Chard; both towns were part of the Bishop's estate.

Wellington town plan based on 1842 map

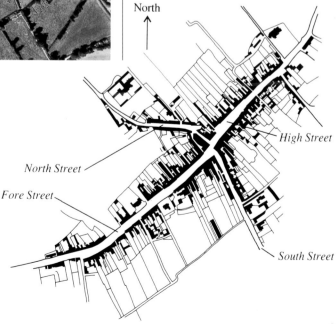

North

North Street

Fore Street

High Street

South Street

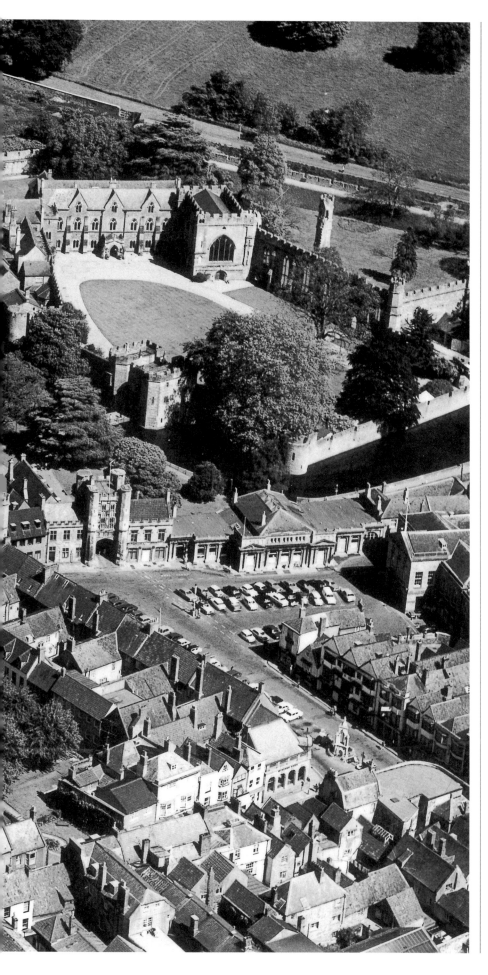

The city of **WELLS** contains one of the finest cathedrals in England. Situated at the foot of the Mendip Hills, the settlement takes its name from the natural springs which rise here just to the east of the Cathedral.

There was a church at Wells in the eighth century and in the tenth century a cathedral was established here. Much of the present building dates to the twelfth century and is on a different alignment from the Anglo-Saxon one. Recent excavations have shown that there was a Christian site here from the end of the Roman period.

This view is dominated by the collection of buildings associated with the cathedral. The cathedral itself has a chapter house (octagonal on the left) and a cloister, (the square on the right) although it was always secular, staffed by canons rather than monks. To the right is the moated, fortified palace of the bishops, still the home of the Bishop of Bath and Wells.

The market place, full of cars in this photograph, was paved in 1993 and this work has completed a substantial enhancement project which links to the Cathedral Green and Vicars Close.

Of all the medieval villages in Somerset, **DUNSTER** with its impressive castle, its wide rectangular market place and Yarn Market, are characteristic of a 'typical English village'. The church was not only used by the villagefolk but was a cell of Bath Abbey. Traces of the cloister together with a large barn and circular dovecote of the priory survive. As at Stogursey and Nether Stowey, the castle and village were linked. A natural hill formed a defensive site and a castle had been constructed here by the time of the Domesday Book in 1086. Much of the castle which survives today was rebuilt in the sixteenth, seventeenth and nineteenth centuries by the Luttrell family who held the castle from the fourteenth century until 1976 when it passed to the National Trust.

Chapter 8
MONASTIC SITES and CASTLES

For many people the characteristic buildings of medieval England are the ruined castle and abbey. Somerset contains several fine examples of both. Many of these sites are away from the main tourist routes and are rarely overcrowded, which adds considerably to their charm and tranquillity.

The most famous monastic site in Somerset is, without doubt, Glastonbury Abbey. Tradition states that it is one of the earliest Christian centres in the county, but no archaeological evidence has confirmed this to date.

At Cleeve Abbey and at Muchelney Abbey, the pleasure of a quiet historic landscape with stone ruins can be appreciated. There are several other minor monastic sites scattered around the county ranging from Athelney Abbey near East Lyng, which has all but disappeared, through to Stavordale Priory which contains a substantial part of the medieval church.

There are more than thirty castles known in the county and like the lesser monastic sites they are frequently small and are rarely visited. They range in size and quality from the motte and bailey earthworks at Over Stowey through to the extensive remains at Farleigh Hungerford or Dunster.

A settlement existed at **STOGURSEY** at the time of the Domesday Book of 1086. This settlement contains several major elements of a medieval rural settlement. The village is broadly sited on a cross roads with a large market place occupying a rectangular plot which has now largely infilled with houses and gardens. At the eastern end of the village is the parish church which occupies part of the site of the twelfth century priory. Other parts of the priory presumably extended in the direction of Priory Farm; the dovecote with its conical roof is just visible on the photograph.

At the southern end of the village down Mill Lane are the extensive earthwork and ruined remains of the castle of Stogursey, first recorded in 1204. It is a good example of a motte and bailey castle with a shell keep. Its moat is fed by water trapped off a stream almost 2km away. Access is by a simple bridge via a gatehouse. In recent years the castle has been extensively repaired by the Landmark Trust and the gatehouse (shown below) is available as a holiday let.

Plan of Stogursey based on 1841 map

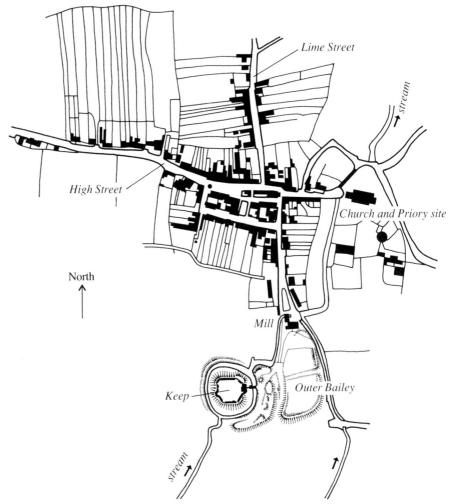

The Carthusian monks from the Grande Chartreuse in France were the most austere of the medieval monastic orders and **WITHAM** was their first priory in England, founded in 1178. Its foundation was supported by Henry II partly in recompense for the murder of Thomas Becket in 1170. There is little to be seen today of the unusual plan of the 'Charterhouse' where each monk lived alone in his own 'cell' or small house with adjacent garden, meeting only for important services in the Church. The photograph shows the earthworks, which cover the fallen stone walls, and shows how the site was built over by two successive houses and their gardens. The site was cut through by the construction of the main West of England railway line in c.1856.

The ruins of **GLASTONBURY ABBEY** may be glimpsed from behind the precinct wall at various points around the town. From the air, however, the large block of open parkland (the former abbey precinct) which contains the ruins of the once influential abbey can clearly be seen.

In the lower part of this photograph the unusual structure of the Abbots' Kitchen indicates the abbey once extended to the current road line. The houses and car park have encroached into the former lands within the abbey precinct, the curving line of Silver Street on the left hand side of the photograph is a good example of this. Recent archaeological excavations to the rear of Glastonbury High Street have shown that a line of an earlier wall and ditch existed in the area to the north (left) of Silver Street. The Great Barn of Glastonbury Abbey, now used as the focus of the Somerset Rural Life Museum, is visible at the top right hand side of the photograph in the area of the modern housing estate.

Within the parkland the extensive parch marks in the grass show the extent of walls and other buried features which show up as lighter patches. This parching phenomenon was particularly clear during the dry summer of 1989.

An engraving of Glastonbury Abbey
ruins in 1733 by S and N Buck

In the north eastern corner of Somerset and cared for by English Heritage are the ruins of **FARLEIGH HUNGERFORD CASTLE**. Situated on a natural rise above the River Frome the two ruinous circular towers and the exposed foundations are all that survive of the defensive part of the castle which was first fortified in 1377 by Sir Thomas Hungerford and his son. In c. 1425 a polygonal outer court was added to the main castle and this survived the ravages of the Civil War but had fallen into disrepair by the early part of the eighteenth century. The chapel was originally the parish church of St Leonard which was incorporated into the manorial enclosure and modified for the personal use of the Hungerford family.

MUCHELNEY ABBEY. The first monastic settlement here has its origins in the Anglo-Saxon period, probably in the seventh century. On the site today the remains of the Abbey church have been laid out and exposed following excavations in the 1950s. The monument and the impressive Abbot's house, which dates from the fifteenth century, are managed by English Heritage and the site is open to the public in the summer months. The very name Muchelney means 'Great Island' and flooding has occurred around Muchelney Abbey and village for many years. It is not exceptional to hear of the island being cut off and for the local farmers to be rescuing cattle from the rapidly rising flood waters of the River Parrett. In the middle ages Muchelney would have been mainly accessible by boat for a substantial part of the year.

Largely hidden away from view on the western side of the failed medieval town of **NETHER STOWEY** is the motte and bailey castle which was probably built by Robert de Chandos in the early twelfth century. It is however possible to visit the top of the earth mound or motte by following a public footpath and the view from the castle is extensive. The earthworks within the central part of the motte mark the position of a substantial stone tower or keep. The thickness of the walls suggests a tower of at least 12 metres in height. Of all the small motte and bailey castles in Somerset this site at Nether Stowey is perhaps the best example of a tower keep making use of a natural hilltop with several surrounding baileys. The castle had been abandoned by 1485 and was known as Castle Hill or Old Castle in 1620.

STAVORDALE PRIORY is one of the best examples of a small monastic church in the county although it has only recently been investigated. The Priory was founded as a house of Augustinian canons of the Victorine group by 1243 and was never very rich nor held an extensive estate. The priory church forms the main part of the current house and much of the existing structure was rebuilt by 1443 by John Stourton. The Priory was merged with Taunton in 1533 and was probably converted into a residence shortly after the reformation. The surviving buildings were restored and extended by the eminent architect Thomas Colcutt in c.1904. The formal landscaped grounds were created in the 1980s. Around the site are earthworks indicating further buildings, fishponds and enclosure banks associated with the priory.

NUNNEY is a small village near Frome, known for its fine example of a late fourteenth century castle, now cared for by English Heritage. The castle is unusual: a tall tower house rather like some of those in Scotland. This was moated and there was probably a bailey or enclosure with other buildings nearby where is now Castle Farm with its large barn (right). The Delamare family constructed the castle in about 1373 reputedly copying the style from French castles. The castle was badly damaged during the Civil War and was not occupied afterwards.

Chapter 9
HOUSES, PARKS and GARDENS

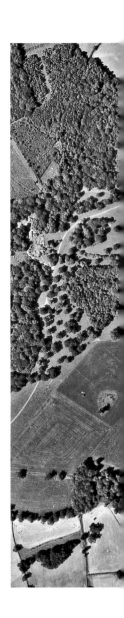

The many important historic houses, parks and gardens in Somerset vary in size from small individual houses and gardens such as Cricket St Thomas, up to the extensive gardens and landscapes around Montacute House. In many examples the ideas of a landscaped house, park and gardens are linked, reflecting the ideas and aspirations of a particular landowner or designer.

In recent years some of these landscapes have been threatened by development - a particularly sad case occurred at Orchardleigh Park near Frome - although not all will remain unaltered, the very nature of development and change within the countryside affects the way in which we look after and utilise our landscape.

Aerial photographs provide an accurate record of the countryside at a particular point in time, in this instance enabling us to see whole 'landscaped' areas, and their value for historic landscape studies has been increasingly used in recent years.

ORCHARDLEIGH House was built between 1855 and 1858 by Thomas Henry Wyatt for William Duckworth (in a mixture of Elizabethan and French chateau styles). The Victorian country house replaced an earlier manor house built to the south of the church of St Mary. The church was left on an island after the village was deserted and the lake built below the house. The gardens and pleasure grounds were laid out by a Mr Page and were one of the best examples of a nineteenth century landscaped garden in the county until a few years ago. The grounds have been seriously affected by development proposals for two large golf courses which went sadly wrong. This aerial photograph taken in 1971 shows the parkland with its fine trees. The restoration and completion of the golf courses will change this landscape for many generations.

DILLINGTON HOUSE is owned by Somerset County Council and serves as a residential Adult Education College. Originally built in the mid-sixteenth century the house was extensively remodelled by James Pennethorne in 1838. The stables and mews were added in 1875 and have been recently converted. The grounds of Dillington House contains some fine specimen trees visible in plan on this photograph.

North

A nineteenth century engraving of Dillington House

BRYMPTON HOUSE at Brympton D'Evercy was sold in 1992 after being in the Fane family since 1731. The house, landscaped gardens and the church of the now deserted medieval village of Brympton form one of the most impressive groups of buildings in the county. When viewed from above it is easy to see how the house has grown up next to the medieval parish church. It is likely that the village of Brympton was cleared away by the D'Evercy or the Sydenham family in the later medieval period. There is no trace of any village-type earthworks visible from the air but traces of ridge and furrow can be seen within the park. The house is not open to the public.

The manor house and wildlife park at **CRICKET ST THOMAS** on the A30 near Chard in south Somerset is one of the major tourist attractions in the county. The house was altered by Sir John Soane and completed by 1807 for Admiral Alexander Hood, Viscount Bridport. The second Lord Bridport gradually demolished Cricket village, diverted roads and built lodges and walls to create an extensive estate. The house was improved from 1898 for F.J. Fry, the chocolate manufacturer. The wildlife park started in 1967 and the house and gardens were used in the television series *'To The Manor Born'*.

North

On the edge of Milborne Port in south-east Somerset stands **VEN HOUSE**, the first substantial brick-built country house in the county. The house was completed in about 1725 for Nathaniel Ireson the mason, builder and pottery manufacturer of Wincanton. In common with many of the grander houses in the county it has not remained in its original form and it was altered and extended by Decimus Burton in 1836. This is a view of the rear of the house showing part of the gardens. It is reported that the clay for the bricks was dug on site and the resultant pits were shaped and filled with water to form part of the landscaping of the grounds.

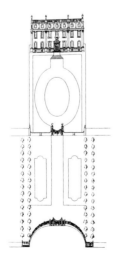

Richard Grange's plan for one of the original gardens

HESTERCOMBE HOUSE. The importance of Hestercombe lies not in the house of the Portman family, built in 1875, but in the splendid garden laid out on the south side. This was begun in 1903 to the designs of the architect Edwin Lutyens. The plan, which can be clearly seen in this air photograph, reflects the formal arrangements of Elizabethan gardens. The planting was by Gertrude Jekyll and Hestercombe is considered to be one of the finest examples of their partnership. The gardens have recently been beautifully restored by Somerset County Council. The house is used as the headquarters of the County Fire Brigade and the gardens are open during working hours and at summer weekends.

Sir Edwin Lutyens's Original Plans of the Garden

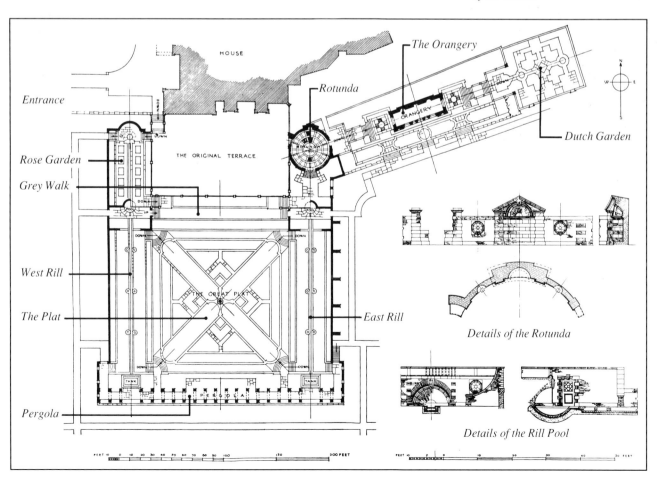

Entrance

Rose Garden

Grey Walk

West Rill

The Plat

Pergola

HOUSE

THE ORIGINAL TERRACE

THE GREAT PLAT

TANK

TANK

PERGOLA

Rotunda

The Orangery

ORANGERY

Dutch Garden

East Rill

Details of the Rotunda

Details of the Rill Pool

FEET 10 0 10 20 30 40 70 60 80 90 100 · · · 150 · · · 200 FEET

FEET 10 5 0 10 20 30 40 50 FEET

The most striking and obvious features of **LOW HAM** medieval village are the isolated church and the extensive post medieval garden earthworks. The church was begun by the Hext family in 1623 and was consecrated in 1669. It has been described as 'one of the most instructive cases of early Gothicism in England' (Pevsner 1958). The aerial photograph clearly shows the earthworks of the garden terraces and the leats that supplied water. A survey of the earthworks has allowed a provisional interpretation of the site into its different periods of activity.

The first house was built, or rebuilt, by Sir Edward Hext around 1590. The regular earthworks to the south-west indicate the formal gardens, but appear to be unfinished. A hundred years later the house was pulled down and work started on the second mansion next to the church. This house was never completed and was in ruins by 1823.

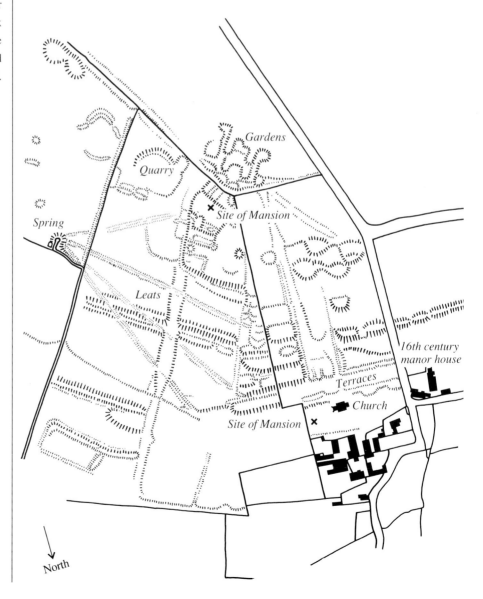

North

In the centre of this parkland is the house known as **MELLS PARK** built in 1925 by Sir Edwin Lutyens for Reginald McKenna, Chairman of the Midland Bank, on the site of an earlier eighteenth century house. The parkland is extensive and is listed as being of national importance in the English Heritage Register of Parks and Gardens. If development proposals for Whatley Quarry are approved then the southern and eastern edge of the park will be removed by quarrying.

The village of **MONTACUTE** is one of the most visited and special of the Ham Stone villages in southern Somerset. This photograph shows four of the main elements of the historic settlement and their relationships to each other. At the top of the photograph standing within its landscaped grounds is Montacute House, an Elizabethan mansion built c.1590 for Sir Edward Phelips. Much of what is visible today has been carefully restored by the National Trust over recent years. In the top right hand part of the photograph there are clear traces of the former open field strips surviving as ridge and furrow earthworks which were incorporated into the landscaped parkland. In the centre of the photograph the curving S shape of the road weaves its way past the parish church of St Catherine, which has some fine Norman stonework, towards the open area of a market place, known locally as The Borough. It was in this area that a small planned market place and burgage plots were laid out, probably in the thirteenth century. At the bottom of the photograph the mainly sixteenth century gatehouse of Montacute Priory can be seen. The large field on the right of the church probably contained the main monastic buildings. All that survives above ground today, apart from the gatehouse, is a square dovecote of medieval date.

An aerial view of Montacute House and grounds

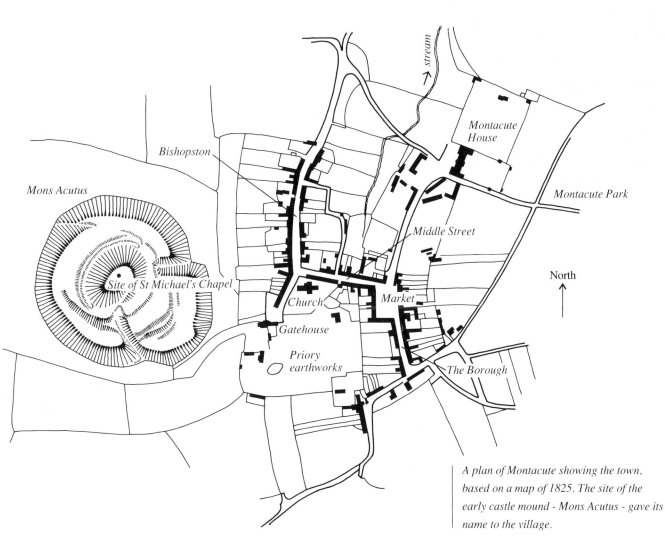

A plan of Montacute showing the town, based on a map of 1825. The site of the early castle mound - Mons Acutus - gave its name to the village.

Chapter 10
COMMUNICATIONS

The geology and landscape of Somerset have influenced the pattern of communications through the centuries which is constantly changing to satisfy the needs of each generation. Many of the ancient roads follow the natural ridge routes across the county above the flooded wetlands. Extensive parts of central Somerset would have been impassable in the winter months and the tradition of timber trackways remained in use for more than 3000 years. Somerset has archaeological evidence of some of the oldest built trackways in the world in the form of the Sweet Track on Shapwick Heath. The Roman Fosse Way cuts across the county on its way from Exeter to Lincoln and is still a major cross country route. There are two main east to west routes through the county, the A303 and the A30, both of which are likely to be partly on ancient roadlines. The construction of the M5 motorway and improvements to the A303 enabled traffic to move swiftly through the county.

Transport using rivers and canals was fairly extensive. The first canal served the Somerset coalfields in the north of the county. Of the main canals the Bridgwater to Taunton canal was opened in 1827 and is currently being repaired to receive boat traffic once again. There were other canals across the county which have now been abandoned and survive largely as earthworks such as the Westport Canal near Ilminster. The Great Western canal was constructed from Taunton to Tiverton (1838-67) and a short-lived canal was built, with considerable difficulty, from Chard to Creech St Michael (1842-1867) where it joined the Bridgwater and Taunton Canal.

The first railway through the county was from Bristol to Exeter which was open by 1843. The Somerset and Dorset Railway was built from Burnham-on-Sea to Poole in Dorset as part of an ambitious rail and boat scheme to link Cardiff with Paris! Other smaller local lines were opened for specific purposes such as the West Somerset Mineral Line which was operational from 1856 until 1923. The modern rail route from Taunton to London through Castle Cary was not opened until 1906.

The railway influenced the tourist trade and development of Burnham-on-Sea and Minehead. Today the East Somerset Railway and the West Somerset Railway provide local tourist attractions for railway enthusiasts.

AXBRIDGE. The old road follows the southern edge of the Mendip Hills. It snakes its way along the hill-side linking together all the medieval villages which grew up along the spring line. Some of these settlements developed into substantial centres in the medieval period such as Axbridge, whereas others such as Compton Bishop remained quiet villages.

The bypass follows the line of the former railway. This road is the main link from the M5 to Cheddar and the City of Wells and is travelled by thousands of tourists in the summer season. This part of the county is famous for its strawberry fields, visible along this southern slope of the Mendip Hills.

MINEHEAD HARBOUR. Minehead is now thought of as a holiday resort but in earlier times it was one of a number of important local ports on this part of the Somerset coast. In the picture the massive curving stone jetty can be seen sheltering a small harbour on the east side. This was developed further to the east initially following the demise of the harbour at Dunster. Minehead Harbour had its heyday in the seventeenth and eighteenth centuries; Gervard in 1633 remarks *'an harbour for ordinary barks much frequented by such as pass to and from Ireland.'* Today a few pleasure trips and fishing boats use the harbour.

WESTONZOYLAND AIRFIELD. This flat fen-like part of Sedgemoor was first used for Air Force summer camps in 1926. Following the outbreak of World War II, Westonzoyland was made a self accounting station on September 1st 1940. Numerous improvements and extensions to the runways and military buildings were made and in 1943 concrete runways were laid. In March of the following year the base was used for the trial of the M3 towed gliders, later to be used during D-Day operations.

In April 1944 more than 2000 personnel were accommodated here with over 100 gliders of the USAAF. The airfield fell out of use after 1946 although not into disrepair. It was reactivated in June 1952 in response to the Korean War. The final RAF squadron left the base in 1957 and the site was sold by the Air Ministry in 1959. Several of the military buildings still survive although most of the runways have been removed.

North

BRIDGWATER DOCKS AND BRICKWORKS

BRIDGWATER DOCKS AND BRICKWORKS. Bridgwater, situated on the River Parrett, had access to the Severn Estuary and developed as a significant local port from medieval times. The main period of growth was in the nineteenth century and in 1841 an inner dock and tidal basin were excavated to the design of Thomas Maddicks. At the western end of the dock a link was made to the Bridgwater and Taunton Canal. A bascule (moveable) bridge and a complicated system of sluices and culverts supplemented by a purpose-designed dredger enabled the Parrett mud to be kept under control. In 1878 the dock complex reached its peak of importance handling over a million tons of goods carried by nearly 4000 ships. Trading continued until after the Second World War. Somerset County Council acquired the docks to ensure their preservation and today the area has been redeveloped for

housing, the docks are used as a marina and Wares Warehouse has been converted into flats, a public house and a restaurant.

On the lower bank of the River Parrett, the chimneys of the former Barhams Brickworks can be clearly seen. This photograph shows the drying sheds and outbuildings associated with this important local industry. Today, only one of the brick kilns survives and this has been restored by Somerset County Council to form the basis of the Somerset Brick and Tile Museum.

Middle: The Docks after redevelopment
Lower: Brick Kiln under restoration in 1991

Yeovilton
Flugplatz

Bild Nr. *F 899b/40./603* Geogr. Lage: 2° 38′ W, 51° 01′ N, Höhe ü. d. M. *21* m   Stand: *II. 47.*

Maßstab etwa 1 : 11 500   (1 cm = 115 m)   Lfl. Kdo. 3

Ⓐ GB 10 334 Flugplatz   1 100 × 800 m

Teil I	1)	4 Hallen	etwa	8 000	qm
======	2)	1 Schuppen	etwa	200	qm
	3)	40 Haus-u.Rundzelte	etwa	500	qm
	4)	Scheinwerferstellung			
	5)	Flakstellungen			
	6)	Abstellplätze für Flugzeuge			
	7)	4 Startbahnen			
		bebaute Fläche	etwa	8 700	qm
Teil II	8)	Unterkunfts- und			
=======		Nebengebäude	etwa	12 000	qm
		Gesamtfläche	etwa	150 000	qm

Ⓑ

GB 20 41 Nachschublager der Luftwaffe

9)	11 Hallen	etwa	25 000	qm
10)	Verwaltungs- und			
	Lagergebäude	etwa	7 000	qm
11)	Halle im Bau			
	bebaute Fläche	etwa	32 000	qm
	Gesamtfläche	etwa	220 000	qm

The earliest known photographs which cover the county date from c.1940-41 when the German Luftwaffe (airforce) flew over most of Britain to obtain target maps. This photograph, taken in 1941, shows **YEOVILTON** in its very early days. The base was established by the Admiralty in 1939 as RNAS Yeovilton and commissioned as HMS Heron on 18 June 1940. The descriptive text describes 4 hangars, 1 shed, 40 marquees and bell tents and other features interpreted by the Germans from the photograph.

WATCHET HARBOUR. There was a Saxon fort or 'burh' at Watchet by the early tenth century and it is now thought that this was at Daw's Castle to the west of the town. The town probably developed in the middle ages along Swain Street and the Market place (in the centre). The western jetty was the terminus of the mineral railway from the iron mines on the Brendon Hills. The eastern jetty was used by the West Somerset Railway and its line can be seen coming in top left, between the houses, towards the jetty. The railway line is now privately run and forms a major tourist attraction in West Somerset.

The **M5 MOTORWAY**, shown here passing Brent Knoll, opened through Somerset in 1976 to link the south west of England into the motorway network. Unlike the earlier route to the south west, the A38, the M5 avoided all towns and villages and cut a broad swathe through the Somerset landscape.

The 1970s was the period which saw the realisation that modern development techniques were destroying historic features and archaeological sites. The archaeological monitoring of construction of the M5 was one of the pioneering examples of this in the country and more than 200 previously unidentified archaeological sites were recorded.

The Brendon Hills are one of the quiet corners of Somerset with gentle rolling hills and numerous scattered hamlets and farms. The construction of the reservoir at **WIMBLEBALL** between 1974 and 1977 by the damming of the Haddeo river, a tributary of the Exe, resulted in the destruction of several farm buildings at Hurscombe, a medieval farm site. Many of the surrounding hedgerows and boundary banks were also destroyed.

The reservoir now supplies most of the water for Taunton, Tiverton and Exeter. The site is managed by South West Water and the reservoir and surrounding land are used for numerous recreational activities such as boating, wind-surfing and walking.

Towards the bottom of this photograph can be seen the settlement of Upton with its ruined medieval church tower.

North

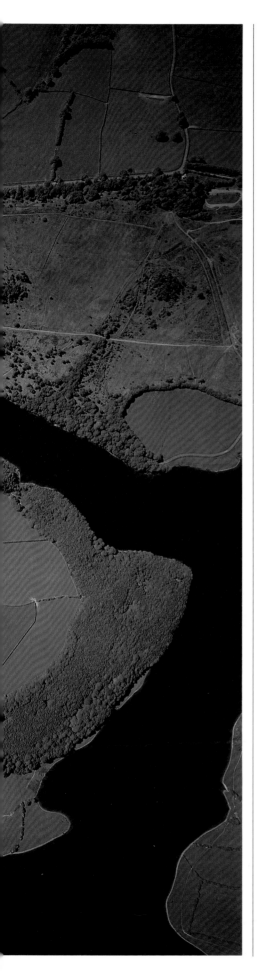

Chapter 11
MODERN LANDSCAPES

Somerset is still a very rural county with agriculture one of the main sources of employment.

There have been several periods of industrialisation and exploitation of the mineral resources within the county and each activity has left its mark. Aerial photographs can be useful to examine and identify these features particularly when they have been neglected or deserted such as the lead mines near Charterhouse on Mendip.

Today, one of the main sources of industrial activity in the county is the extraction of limestone from the eastern Mendips. This has resulted in the extensive removal and reshaping of the countryside over many years and this is set to continue on several sites well into the next century. The quarrying industry forms an important part of the economy of the county.

Modern buildings and developments in and around our historic towns and villages has been relatively modest in recent years. The phenomenon of the Business Park and the out of town shopping complex has started to arrive and examples can be seen at Bridgwater, Taunton and Yeovil.

The first reactor at Hinkley Point Nuclear Power Station was built in 1965 and an application for a third station has already been approved by the Department for Energy. The planning approval gives permission for the site to be developed, provided that the political desire for nuclear energy continues and that work starts before 1998.

Managing the countryside with conservation in mind is currently receiving substantial government support. Many of the rural areas such as the Somerset Levels and Moors and Exmoor are being managed to create and maintain a 'modern' but 'conserved' rural landscape.

In the north eastern corner of Somerset the extensive deposits of limestone are currently being excavated to supply hard rock to the construction industry. The extraction of limestone in this area has been going on for many hundreds of years and several quarry sites have been in use for many generations. **WHATLEY QUARRY** is one of the largest in Britain with more than 5 million tonnes of stone being removed each year. It is proposed to extend this quarry to cover an area of more than 200 hectares. Stone from Somerset is exported by road and rail to various centres around the country. The close-up photograph shows the processing plant within the quarry.

This part of the northern coast line of Somerset is dominated by the massive blocks of **HINKLEY POINT POWER STATION**. The first nuclear reactor was built here in 1965 and this photograph shows the construction work under way for Hinkley 'B' which opened in 1976. The power station provided 13 terrawatt hours of electricity in 1992.

On the east side of Minehead, **BUTLINS HOLIDAY CAMP** represents a stage in the development of holiday accommodation in the 1940s and 1950s when families could travel to the seaside relatively cheaply living in barrack-like buildings. The railway brought in the holiday makers and the beach was to hand for play and bathing. With changing holiday fashions the railway now only operates as a tourist line and the holiday camp has been renamed Somerwest World and is one of the leading holiday resorts in the West Country. The two photographs illustrate how the site has changed over the past thirty years or so. This false colour infra-red taken in 1992 shows the new road system put in to serve Minehead.

SOURCES

The following list of sources and collections provides further information on the wide range of aerial photographs available for the county.

SOMERSET

LOCAL HISTORY LIBRARY,
Taunton Castle, Taunton TA1 4AD
Tel: (0823) 288871. (Closed Mondays).
1946-8 RAF vertical photographs at
approximately 1:10560 scale
c.1960-70 oblique black & white (B/W)
photographs of towns and villages.

SOMERSET COUNTY COUNCIL,
Sites and Monuments Record,
Environment Department,
County Hall, Taunton TA1 4DY
Tel:(0823) 255426 for appointment.
Miscellaneous 35mm colour slides of the
county c.1975-93
Several hundred B/W oblique photographs
c.1970 onwards
To view B/W or colour verticals held by
SCC Tel: (0823) 255628 for appointment
1971 B/W vertical air photography at
1:10,000 scale
1981 B/W vertical air photography at
1:10,000 scale
1992 colour vertical air photography at
1:25,000 scale

SOMERSET COUNTY ARCHIVE &
RECORD SERVICE,
Obridge Road, Taunton, TA2 7PU
Tel: (0823) 337600 for appointment
c.1970 1:2500 scale B/W vertical
enlargements of parts of the county

EXMOOR NATIONAL PARK,
Exmoor House, Dulverton,
Somerset TA22 9HL
Tel: (0398) 23665 for appointment.
B/W vertical air photograph c.1970-1992
False colour Infra-Red photography of
Exmoor National Park c.1980-1992.

ENGLISH NATURE,
Roughmoor, Bishops Hull,
Taunton TA1 5AA
Tel: (0823) 283211 for appointment.
B/W vertical air photography 1980 onwards
of various parts of the county.

MINISTRY OF AGRICULTURE,
FISHERIES AND FOODS,
Quantock House, Paul Street,
Taunton TA1 3NX.
Tel: (0823) 337922 for appointment.
B/W vertical air photographs of parts of the
county, particularly Environmentally
Sensitive Areas such as the Somerset Levels
and Moors.

OUT OF COUNTY

ROYAL COMMISSION ON THE
HISTORICAL MONUMENTS OF
ENGLAND,
National Air Photograph Collection,
Alexander House, 19 Fleming Way,
Swindon Wilts, SN1 2NG.
Tel: (0793) 414100 for appointment.
B/W verticals and obliques and some 35mm
colour slides.

CAMBRIDGE UNIVERSITY
COLLECTION OF AERIAL
PHOTOGRAPHS,
Mond Building, Free School Lane,
Cambridge CB2 3RF.
Tel: (0223) 337733 for details.
B/W only verticals and obliques from
c.1950 onwards.

COMMERCIAL SUPPLIERS

WEST AIR PHOTOGRAPHY,
40 Alexandra Parade,
Weston-Super-Mare, Avon BS23 1QZ
Tel: (0934) 621333.

AEROFILMS LTD,
Gate Studio, Station Road,
Borehamwood, Herts WD6 1EJ
Tel: (081) 207 0666.

GEONEX UK LTD,
92-94 Church Road,
Mitcham, Surrey.
Tel: (081) 685 9393.

BIBLIOGRAPHY

GENERAL AERIAL PHOTOGRAPHY

Riley D. (1987) *Air Photography and Archaeology* (Duckworth)

St Joseph J K S (ed.) (1977) *The Uses of Air Photography* (Black, 2nd ed.)

Wilson D R (1982) *Air Photo Interpretation for Archaeologists* (Batsford)

Griffith F (1988) *Devon's Past - An Aerial View* (Devon Books)

Platt C (1984) *Medieval Britain from the Air* (Guild, London)

Muir R (1983) *History from the Air* (Michael Joseph, London)

NAPLIB (1993) *Directory of Aerial Photography Collections in the United Kingdom* (London)

ARCHAEOLOGICAL AND HISTORIC SITES FROM THE AIR

The Cambridge University Committee for Air Photography has published several volumes of aerial photographs which have been accompanied by very full and descriptive essays and captions. These books provide a useful resource for anyone interested in examining and using aerial photographs.

Brown R Allen (1989) *Castles from the Air* (Cambridge)

Knowles D and St Joseph J K S (1952) *Monastic Sites from the Air* (Cambridge)

Beresford M W and St Joseph (1958, 2nd ed. 1979) *Medieval England - An Aerial Survey* (Cambridge)

Frere S S and St Joseph J K S (1983) *Roman Britain from the Air* (Cambridge)

Hudson K (1984) *Industrial History from the Air* (Cambridge)

Glasscock R (ed) (1992) *Historic Landscapes of Britain from the Air* (Cambridge)

Stevens N (ed) (1990) *Natural Landscapes of Britain from the Air* (Cambridge)

Bayliss-Smith T and Owens S (ed) (1990) *Britain's Changing Environment from the Air* (Cambridge)

Darvill T C (1986) *The Archaeology of the Uplands* (RCHME and CBA)

Whimster R (1989) *The Emerging Past - Air Photography and the Buried Landscape* (RCHME, London)

Palmer R and Cox C (1993) *Uses of Aerial Photography in Archaeological Evaluations* (Institute of Field Archaeologists Technical Paper Number 12, Birmingham)

SOMERSET ARCHAEOLOGY AND HISTORY

For a detailed historical description of the county the definitive work is published in the volumes of the *Victoria County History*. Six volumes have been published up to 1993 covering various parts of the county and these should be used as the first reference point for historical research at the parish level. Aerial photographs are rarely used in these volumes but historic landscape maps can be readily compared with early aerial photographs - often to good effect.

There are several introductory books on the history and archaeology of the county the following is a selection of several which use aerial photographs.

Adkins L and Adkins R (1992) *A Field Guide to Somerset Archaeology* (Dovecote)

Aston M (ed) (1988) *Aspects of the Medieval Landscape of Somerset* (SCC Taunton)

Aston M and Burrow I (1982) *The Archaeology of Somerset* (SCC Taunton)

Aston M and Leech R (1977) *Historic Towns in Somerset* (CRAAGS, Bristol)

Bush R and Comrie J (1989) *Somerset - A portrait in Colour* (Dovecote)

Dunning R (1978) *A History of Somerset* (Somerset County Council)

Dunning R (1983) *A History of Somerset* (Phillimore)

Dunning R (1980) *Somerset and Avon* (Bartholmew, Edinburgh)

Dunning R (1992) *Bridgwater - A History and Guide* (Alan Sutton)

Ellison A (1983) *Medieval Villages in SE Somerset* (Western Archaeological Trust)

Fletcher K (1991) *The Somerset Levels and Moors* (SCC Taunton)

Havinden M (1981) *The Somerset Landscape* (Hodder, London)

Hawkins M (1988) *Somerset at War 1939-1945* (Dovecote)

Pevsner N (1958a) *North Somerset and Bristol* (Penguin)

Pevsner N (1958b) *South and West Somerset* (Penguin)

Siraut M, Dunning R and Brown K (1992) *The Quantocks - A Past Worth Preserving* (Somerset Books)

Williams M (1970) *The Draining of the Somerset Levels.* (Cambridge)